Brandon Bartlett
Jesse K. Miguel
Phillip Miller
Adam Noble
Todd Peterson
Martha Rowlett

Web Site Authors:
Eric Brunkow
Greg Phillips

New Riders Publishing, Indianapolis, Indiana

3D Studio® Architectural Rendering

By Brandon Bartlett, Jesse K. Miguel, Phillip Miller, Adam Noble, Todd Peterson, and Martha Rowlett

Web Site Authors: Eric Brunkow and Greg Phillips

Published by:
New Riders Publishing
201 West 103rd Street
Indianapolis, IN 46290 USA

Printed in the United States of America 1 2 3 4 5 6 7 8 9 0

CIP Available Upon Request

Warning and Disclaimer

This book is designed to provide information about the 3D Studio computer program. Every effort has been made to make this book as complete and as accurate as possible, but no warranty or fitness is implied.

The information is provided on an "as is" basis. The author(s) and New Riders Publishing shall have neither liability nor responsibility to any person or entity with respect to any loss or damages arising from the information contained in this book or from the use of the disks or programs that may accompany it.

Publisher	Don Fowley
Publishing Manager	David Dwyer
Marketing Manager	Mary Foote
Managing Editor	Carla Hall

This book was produced digitally by Macmillan Computer Publishing and manufactured by Shepard Poorman Communications Corporation, Indianapolis, Indiana.

Trademark Acknowledgments

All terms mentioned in this book that are known to be trademarks or service marks have been appropriately capitalized. New Riders Publishing cannot attest to the accuracy of this information. Use of a term in this book should not be regarded as affecting the validity of any trademark or service mark.

New Riders Publishing

The staff of New Riders Publishing is committed to bringing you the very best in computer reference material. Each New Riders book is the result of months of work by authors and staff who research and refine the information contained within its covers.

As part of this commitment to you, the NRP reader, New Riders invites your input. Please let us know if you enjoy this book, if you have trouble with the information and examples presented, or if you have a suggestion for the next edition.

Please note, though: New Riders staff cannot serve as a technical resource for 3D Studio or for questions about software- or hardware-related problems. Please refer to the documentation that accompanies 3D Studio or to the applications' Help systems.

If you have a question or comment about any New Riders book, there are several ways to contact New Riders Publishing. We will respond to as many readers as we can. Your name, address, or phone number will never become part of a mailing list or be used for any purpose other than to help us continue to bring you the best books possible. You can write us at the following address:

> New Riders Publishing
> Attn: Publisher
> 201 W. 103rd Street
> Indianapolis, IN 46290

If you prefer, you can fax New Riders Publishing at (317) 581-4670.

You can also send electronic mail to New Riders at the following Internet address:

ddwyer@newriders.mcp.com

NRP is an imprint of Macmillan Computer Publishing. To obtain a catalog or information, or to purchase any Macmillan Computer Publishing book, call (800) 428-5331.

Thank you for selecting *3D Studio Architectural Rendering*!

Product Director
Alicia Buckley

Development Editor
John Kane

Project Editor
Amy Bezek

Copy Editors
Geneil Breeze
Phil Worthington

Technical Editor
Eric Peterson

Associate Marketing Manager
Tamara Apple

Acquisitions Coordinator
Stacey Beheler

Publisher's Assistant
Karen Opal

Cover Designer
Karen Ruggles

Cover Illustration
Martha Rowlett

Cover Production
Aren Howell

Book Designer
Anne Jones

Production Manager
Kelly Dobbs

Production Team Supervisor
Laurie Casey

Graphics Image Specialists
Brad Dixon
Sonja Hart
Todd Wente

Production Analysts
Jason Hand
Bobbi Satterfield

Production Team
Heather E. Butler
Kim Cofer
Joe Millay
Erika Millen
Christine Tyner
Scott Tullis

Indexer
Tom Dinse

Contents at a Glance

Bonus Chapters on the New Riders Web Site

**New Riders has placed two bonus chapters on its World Wide Web home-
page at**

`http://www.mcp.com/newriders`

**"Interior Lighting," by Greg Phillips, shows the 3D Studio user how to cre-
ate dynamic lighting effects from single and multiple light sources, such as
lamps, spot, fluorescence, display lights, and reflection lighting. "Site
Planning," by Eric Brunkow, is an example of how 3D Studio can be used to
help visualize a site to further aid in the understanding of its appearance
and design.**

**Each of these is the equivalent of an entire chapter from this book. All of
the explanatory text and accompanying figures can be accessed by pointing
your Web browser to this URL:**

`http://www.mcp.com/newriders/gm/index.html`

Check them out!

Table of Contents

Introduction:

Architectural Rendering and the Design Process

by Phillip Miller, 3D Studio MAX Product Manager

Although this book is entitled *3D Studio Architectural Rendering,* and much of its emphasis is on creating visuals, it is actually about a tool that considerably aids the design process. Using computer graphics to examine every aspect of a design, explore a myriad of options, or stroll through a space while it is still a proposal goes far beyond what is possible with traditional methods of rendering and presentation. While it's true that this book guides you in creating photorealistic renderings and animations, it is the process of their creation that is the real value to the designer. Although renderings shown to clients may seem like the final results to them, the design evolution that occurred during their creation is often much more valuable to the architects and beneficial to the designs themselves. Architects are not creating renderings as much as they are *visualizing* their designs. The result is no longer just a presentation drawing—it is a *visualization* of what that design is, might, or could be.

Visualization

Visualization is *not* new. It's a tradition that can be traced to back to the first time anyone ever graphically described a concept, thought, or design— perhaps the wheel? What *is* new are the tools with which architects can explore and express their designs. The designer's tools for visualization have been limited to hand sketches and scale models for thousands of years. Today, new tools, such as photorealistic renderings, walkthroughs, and dynamic sections, are suddenly available and bring with them visualization opportunities that were only dreamed of a few years ago. What 3D Studio does is make these tools usable and affordable to every design professional, and on equipment that is readily available.

Computer visualization is not eliminating the traditional sketch or model, although it does limit the designer's dependence on them. Although sketches and models are valuable tools in their own right, they take considerable time to create, and once made are not easily changed. Wanting to see a different finish or seeing a space from another viewpoint means an entirely new drawing. With 3D Studio, however, it's a simple material redefinition or camera move. Wanting to see a different roof slope means a new model, and seeing within the structure means the creation of a sectioned interior model (the most time-consuming of all to produce). With 3D Studio adjusting a roof is often just a matter of moving vertices, and experiencing the defined space is as basic as moving the camera inside or adjusting its clipping plane.

Visualization is nearly always enabling us to see something that is not normally possible. The most common reason for a visualization, and the emphasis of this book, is to describe a proposed design or concept. Yet a visualization could be of what no longer exists (re-creating lost buildings and cities), of what is not normally possible to see (viewing a 3D building section or subterranean condition), or of what is easier to describe abstractly (comparing building program volumes or the timed sequence of construction).

Those doing visualization, while being quite proud of their renderings and animations, usually do not consider this output to be what they *really* do. Architectural renderings and walkthroughs enable architects to analyze their designs and then convince clients of the design's merit. They are tools with which to do their work better, and not ends in themselves. Throughout the visualization process there is little confusion that the architecture is always the final product. In the end, it's the buildings and the spaces that are judged as a measure of those that created and designed them. The conceptual images that aided in their design, and the presentation images that won their approval, were tools in the early process of building the project.

3D Studio and the Design Process

Architectural visualization has always been integral to the design process. Computer design tools such as 3D Studio radically change the depth to which visualization occurs at each stage in the process. The point and frequency with which a designer uses 3D Studio varies according to personal preference, needs, and skill. What is evident among those designers fluent in 3D Studio is the extent to which it is permeating every design stage. Ideas can simply be explored to a greater degree, and most often faster, with 3D Studio than by using traditional methods.

Conceptual Design

For architects, perhaps the most important use for 3D Studio visualization is in choosing the best approach for their design. Many feel this is where visualization aids the most, allowing them to fully evaluate their design concepts, show potential problems, and explore permutations or new ideas. 3D Studio enables designers to investigate these early designs to a higher degree than ever before possible—they can be more confident and prepared at the earliest stages. The conceptual massing can be viewed from every angle in true perspective, toured from within, and examined in context with their eventual surroundings.

The first stage of the design process is often termed conceptual: the designer is brainstorming and coming up with numerous options from various directions while investigating their opportunities and validity. The obstacle facing a designer is the time it takes to adequately investigate the numerous concepts. A sketch, even a perspectively correct one, is just a two-dimensional abstract. Numerous sketches, and often scale models, need to be made for designers to adequately investigate and finally convince themselves of an approach. The most dangerous thing a designer can do is present a bad design option to a client. At best, presenting a poor design lowers the client's opinion for the designer; at worst, the client may choose to proceed with the poor design proposal over the good ones!

Design is nearly always a balance of art and science. Although a design strives to be appealing and artistic, it also has to work. Design usually begins loose and firms up as it approaches reality. An unfortunate fact is that dramatic design often has to give in to functional or structural reality, because design is easier to change than context or engineering principles. Computer visualization can be a great aid by enabling designers to accurately grapple with reality whenever they wish. Even the earliest concept model can be compared to its context and incorporate its structure or mechanical components.

Presenting the Design

Once convinced on a design direction, designers can enhance the visualization to any required level to convey their design intent to the client for approval. The client is actually whoever passes approval judgment on a design. It may be a traditional client paying a design fee, a design build contractor, a developer trying in turn to convince tenants, an approval board, or even the public at large.

In the past presenting architectural designs had been difficult because clients are not usually skilled in reading what are actually abstract drawings (adjacency diagrams, schematics, plans, elevations, and the most difficult to understand: sections). Basic education on how to read drawings has traditionally become an essential part of many architectural presentations. Perspective sketches and scale models have proven the most communicative tools in the past, but these take an immense amount of time to create and are usually time and/or cost prohibitive during the early design stages.

Computer visualization has been shown to significantly lower the design communication barrier. Clients can see, even experience, a proposal and judge it on merits that they readily understand. Some designers make the computer, and 3D Studio, part of their actual presentation. New views can be seen and options explored with the client through a real-time design investigation.

Every designer experiments to arrive at the right design. The early design phases are often full of bizarre and radical approaches, because only from such a viewpoint can originality progress. Most often these very original strokes are tamed, yet sometimes they live. The chance of a radical direction succeeding is nearly equal to the skill with which it is presented. One reason that radical designs are rarely adopted and produced is that clients have extreme difficulty in picturing that in which they do not have context. A 3D Studio visualization can provide this insight and be an invaluable aid in gaining a client's acceptance of the avant garde.

Selling What Doesn't Exist

A very common and practical use of 3D Studio visualization is to advertise what is still only a proposal. Clients may be passing judgment on the design for their purposes, but often they have to convince others in their own presentations. A visualized design of the proposal often is essential if the project is ever to see completion. A common situation is when developers need to lease so much space or sell a certain number of units before receiving the financing necessary to proceed with the project.

Although this has traditionally been done with "artist sketches," 3D Studio allows the visualized design to evolve into the required images and thus an additional service offered by the designer. The visualization can also be taken to new levels and accommodate custom requests relatively rapidly. Showing the resulting views from any particular balcony on a proposed high-rise, the spatial feeling of a build out in a proposed space, the custom surface treatment for an interested buyer, or the impact of signage from a prime tenant are made very easy by 3D Studio while increasing the architect's value to the development process as well.

Correct Visualization

Often a design can be visualized correctly only if a scale mock-up or, now, a computer visualization is performed. The use of sample boards, the traditional focus of nearly every interior design proposal, is a classic situation. Such presentation boards are usually carefully composed samples of the chosen finishes and clipped photographs of proposed elements (furniture, lighting fixtures, hardware, and so on).

Several problems exist for the interior designer and especially the client. First, the samples are rarely in proportion to eventual reality (the rubber base sample is often larger than the wall's paint swatch.) Second, elements are not depicted in quantity (one chair may look striking while a hundred may appear ridiculous). Third, elements cannot be placed in context (the sofa fabric and carpet samples may work wonderfully together but they may be in different rooms). Finally, finishes are almost always in the abstract (the picture of the chair is placed next to a fabric swatch and a wood-finish sample with the client having to imagine the combined result). In reality, even seasoned designers have difficulty visualizing these combinations in such abstract and are often surprised with the final installation.

3D Studio visualization can take the guesswork from the design process and the makes the presentation of the decisions far easier. Seeing the space with the proposed finishes and furnishings, in context, with appropriate lighting and fixtures, tells without questions whether the composition is correct and speeds approval of the proposal immensely. It can prove what at first seems to be too bold or garish to actually be striking and very appropriate. It also can prevent some embarrassing design blunders.

Exploring "What If?"

The ultimate value at any design stage is the ability to explore "what if?". What if the building were this color, or brick, or metal? What if it were reoriented to face the sunset? What if the ceiling were two feet higher? What if the floor tile were run at an angle? The list is endless and whether the questions are be coming from fellow designers, clients, or contractors, the results often can be viewed in minutes in 3D Studio. The ease with which what-if scenarios can be played out often leads to design investigations that otherwise would not have occurred. Of course, many of these explorations are fruitless, but many shed light on wonderful new approaches that might otherwise have gone untried.

It's a common assumption that CAD and computer renderings automate so much of the architect's job that they should finish projects in less time. While this may be true in some cases, in reality it is not often the case. When given faster design tools, architects and designers simply tend to investigate more design opportunities. On average, projects end up taking the same amount of time to complete as they did by manual methods, although many more design what-ifs are usually explored from initial conception through furniture specification, and the designs most often benefit from it.

Signing Off

Once 3D Studio images have aided in exploring a design, and the photorealistic versions pleased a client, they are sometimes used for approval and reference purposes. This may confirm the client's final acceptance of the design or even the contractor's understanding of the design intent. Those responsible for construction develop a better understanding of what is expected when they see an accurate image and can adjust their bids accordingly and plan their construction correctly. Similarly, the client is well aware of what they are approving, and the chances of changing things during construction due to the surprise of what was not understood is lessened. Accurate visualizations can thus actually reduce costs by reducing expensive change orders, or at the very least establishing what had been agreed upon.

Architectural Visualization's Future

3D Studio Release 4 has proved to be a very valuable tool for designers world-wide, yet it is really just the beginning. If the analogy is made to the motion-picture industry, we are still in the silent era, and the thought of what the visualization equivalent of today's special-effects blockbusters will be is as hard to imagine as *Toy Story* might have been to the Keystone Cops. It's very possible that the distinction between visualization, virtual reality, and CAD will disappear into a spontaneous world of immersive design and digital clay. It's also very likely that the results of computer visualization will become true artistic expressions as designers and artists demand personality over photorealism.

What can be seen today are trends in technology, price, software, relevance, and acceptance. Some things are clear: technology will continue to escalate in capabilities, the cost of professional systems will remain constant yet their power will grow substantially, computer design tools will become incredibly interactive and intuitive, specialized tools for every conceivable need will eventually be available, animation and sound will become integral and expected in presentations, and nearly everything you can touch, see, or hear will be available digitally. While you can see the beginnings of this future in 3D Studio Release 4 today, you will be witnessing much more of it in the next generation of design tools—the first being 3D Studio MAX for Windows NT—very soon.

Phillip Miller
3D Studio MAX Product Manager
Autodesk Multimedia

Modeling

by Jesse K. Miguel, AIA

Boston, Massachusetts

Author Bio

Jesse K. Miguel is a Project Designer/Architectural CAD Coordinator for the architectural/engineering firm of HNTB in Boston, Massachusetts. He is in charge of 3D design on the computer, using Autodesk's AutoCAD and 3D Studio to create 3D computer models for photorealistic still images and computer animation. He is also responsible for overseeing the AutoCAD operations, setting project standards, creating CAD files, and serving as the Architectural Group's CAD client contact. Jesse has recently been named the 3D Rendering and Animation Manager for HNTB at their Kansas City, Missouri, corporate headquarters, where he will be directing the development of 3D computer graphics and animation in the Technical Computer Support Group of HNTB, as well as providing development support for 3D Design for HNTB's 33 design offices throughout the country.

Jesse is a registered architect for the state of Massachusetts and is a member of the American Institute of Architecture, the National Council of the Architectural Registration Board, the Boston Society of Architects, the 3D Studio User's Group of Boston, and the North American Autodesk User's Group. His 3D computer models were featured in *Computer Graphics World*. He holds advanced degrees in architecture from Washington University in St. Louis, and the Massachusetts Institute of Technology (M.I.T.) in Cambridge, Massachusetts.

Chapter Overview

Most architects use AutoCAD as a 2D drafting tool but have not utilized the 3D modeling capabilities inside AutoCAD. Yet more and more classes are being taught in 3D modeling, as the need increases to create 3D models for design purposes, to create realistic rendered models, and finally, to animate the model for walking through the proposed design.

This chapter will discuss the following:

- ◆ Types of 3D modeling used in AutoCAD

- ◆ Viewing in 3D in AutoCAD

- ◆ Tools and methods for building 3D models in AutoCAD

- ◆ A modeling exercise using AutoCAD and 3D Studio to build a famous architectural monument

AutoCAD 3D Modeling

Architectural and engineering AutoCAD users have generally drawn in 2D; this is due to preparing a set of construction documents (formerly known as "blueprints"), which are used for constructing buildings, bridges, and highways. Modeling in 3D has usually been done by constructing a small scale version of a structure for design or presentation purposes for clients and the general public. Perspectives prior to computers were drafted out in 2D, using a certain viewpoint, vanishing points, and horizon lines (quite a painstaking process) to generate a single view. For every different viewpoint, another perspective had to be constructed.

Most, but not all, designers can "visualize" their designs in 3D, in order to translate their ideas into 2D drawings. Some designers, however, think in 2D first and have a difficult time visualizing their design in 3D. For some, physically constructing a small scale 3D model of their design provides them with a visualization tool. The problem with a small scale model is the size; unless the model is full scale (which would be expensive because the final product is to be the full scale model), it's hard to visualize what the building and the spaces look and feel like. Walking through the model would be difficult unless a miniature physical camera could move through the building. Unless you are creating a Hollywood blockbuster with a huge multimillion dollar budget for building elaborate models and using moving cameras, there is no simple way to experience walking through the small scale model.

The use of CAD software to create 2D drawings became an asset in moving from the hand-drafted methods of creating construction drawings. CAD software provided the capability to make numerous changes and revisions without excessive "erasing" and redrafting of the construction drawings. Unfortunately, the majority of architectural AutoCAD users are stuck in the 2D mode. Of the courageous few who venture into 3D land, those who have the ability to visualize in 3D will have a better understanding of creating 3D models. Another approach is to imagine the same process you must do in "building" a 3D model. Depending on what scale model (1/4" scale, 1"=100'-0"), you must think about how a particular part of the model should be built and how much detail to put into it.

This chapter discusses creating 3D models from a 2D drawing file that forms the base of the 3D model. The assumption is that readers of this book are familiar with using AutoCAD in 2D, as a basis for drawing construction plans, elevations, sections, and details—in other words, for generating a set of plans used for construction purposes. Readers are therefore familiar with creating 2D drawings such as the LINE, PLINE, ARC, or ELLIPSE commands; setting up layers (American Institute of Architecture CAD layering standards); creating wblocks and xrefs (external refernences); and using the UCS (User Coordinate System) command to correspond to the setup of the 2D drawing.

Types of Modeling

There are three different types of three-dimensional modeling:

- **Wireframes.** Basically, lines are connected and created in the x, y, and z coordinates to represent a 3D model. A wireframe is similar to a steel frame, the "skeleton" of a building, without any cladding such as brick, glazing, and so on. A wireframe has no surfaces, and you cannot do a Hidden line command

- **Surface models.** A surface model consists of the "skin" of the building or the sheet metal of a car. This is similar to a cardboard box with nothing inside. Surface models are also called *3D meshes*; 3D Studio works most with surface models to generate still images and animation. AutoCAD's Region modeler and 3D meshes create surface models.

- **Solid models.** As the term states, a solid model is a solid mass such as a piece of brick or blocks that has surface and density. Solid models are used in AutoCAD's AME (Advanced Modeling Extension), in AutoCAD Release 13's Solid Modeling feature, or Autodesk's AutoSurf. Solid models are useful for creating models requiring mass properties, and are useful for manufacturing parts. Solid models brought into 3D Studio need to be changed into 3D surfaces.

Depending on the discipline you work in, for 3D Studio, surface or solid modeling is adequate for the use of 3D AutoCAD modeling. In architectural modeling, surface modeling may be adequate for the certain parts of a 3D architectural model that are thin surfaces, such as a tensile curved roofs, canopies, or even walls without openings. Solid modeling is adequate for creating openings such as windows in a wall, unifying parts of walls together. In mechanical engineering for building parts to be manufactured, solid modeling is a necessity. Solid models using AME in AutoCAD Release 11 or 12, or AutoCAD Release 13's Solid Modeler, are ideal for the these types of modeling. The disadvantage of using solid modeling for architectural models is that the file sizes become enourmous, due to the information regarding the properties of the solid model, such as density or weight, that is irrevelant for architectural models. 3D Studio does not need all that extra information; the 3DS file created from an Autocad 3D solid model is much smaller in file size.

Layer Setup for Creating Objects for 3D Studio

Layering conventions for architectural practices usually follow the American Institute of Architects CAD layering guidelines. Constructed lines for 2D drawings are usually set by type; that is, A-WALL, with additional modifiers to differentiate various types of the object (A-WALL-EXTR, A-WALL-PRHT). These layers were developed for the different disciplines in the construction industry (architectural, structural, mechanical, electrical, civil). For 3D design, however, it is wise to create layers that correspond to the type of material the objects will ultimately be made of. Table 1.1 illustrates the layering setup for 2D versus 3D.

Table 1.1 Layering Conventions for 2D and 3D	
2D Layering (per AIA CAD Standards)	*Description*
A-WALL-EXTR	Exterior wall lines
A-WALL-INTR	Interior wall lines
A-WALL-PRHT	Partial walls
A-DOOR	Doors
3D Layering (for 3D Studio objects)	*Description*
WALL01	Exterior walls - Brick
WALL02	Exterior walls - Granite
WALL03	Interior walls - Drywall
DOOR01	Glass exterior doors
DOOR02	Interior wood doors

It should be noted that AutoCAD layering setup was created to provide for 2D drawings and is geared toward plotting out to a final hard copy output and related to plotting configurations. 3D Studio, however, is object-oriented rather than layer-oriented. Instead of creating lines using layers in AutoCAD,

3D Studio creates objects. Therefore, the layering convention for converting 3D AutoCAD objects using the DXFOUT command (or 3DSOUT in AutoCAD Release 13) into 3D Studio should be prepared as if they are objects. 3D Studio does give an option of bringing DXF files from AutoCAD by layer, by object, or by color (see figs. 1.1 and 1.2).

Figure 1.1

Axonometric view of plan with 3D exterior walls.

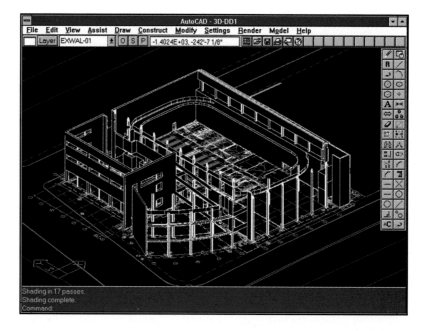

Figure 1.2

Axonometric view with 3D exterior walls and mullions.

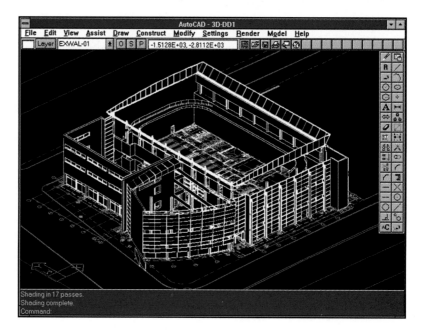

Using Xrefs for Base Floor Plans

Because most architectural users should be familiar with drafting in AutoCAD for 2D, plans, elevations, and sections are usually generated before the building of a detailed 3D CAD model. The drawing file for the first floor plan serves as the base for the 3D model drawing file. The 3D drawing file can be created by copying the existing floor plan and changing and renaming all layers for 3D layering by using the File/New command on the pull-down menu. But because the floor plan will change frequently during the design process, the 3D model must be updated every time the plan changes. A better method is to use Xrefs in the floor plans of the building as a base for the 3D model. Therefore, any change or updates to the floor plans will be referenced in the 3D model, to allow coordination to changes.

The first floor plan drawing file is a good start for creating a base for the 3D model. In AutoCAD, begin by copying the first floor plan to a new file for model building (for example, 3D-BLDG.DWG), erasing all the contents of the existing floor plan, and referencing the first floor plan using the XREF command, at insertion point 0,0,0. This ensures the same limits, units, and UCS settings for the base. Use the Xref command to insert additional floor plans at insertion points 0,0,(floor height of level); for example, the second floor plan at elevation 16'-0" should be inserted at 0,0,16' (see fig. 1.3).

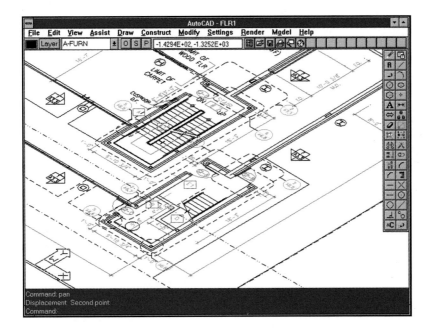

Figure 1.3

Multiple floor plans xrefs in 3D base drawing.

Elevations and sections can also be brought in through xrefs or wblocks. Inserting them into the AutoCAD 3D base drawing file would require setting up the UCS to correspond to the particular side of the building or model, which will be discussed later in the chapter.

Beginning the 3D AutoCAD Model

Prior to building 3D objects, you need to know and understand the following AutoCAD commands:

◆ Setting up mutiple viewports to view the 3D model from various views, such as plan, elevation, isometric, and perspective

◆ Creating isometric and axonometric views using the DDVPOINT command

◆ Using the DVIEW command to create perspective camera views, adjust the lens, and establish camera targets and location

◆ Understanding the UCS (User Coordinate System) command, and how to manipulate it to align a "working surface" for object creation

◆ Knowing the commands or tools to build the actual 3D objects; using 3D faces, thickness, and the CHPROP commands; surface modeling and solid modeling

Viewing in 3D

AutoCAD users working in 2D plans and elevations have been "viewing" their drawing files in 3D. That is, the drawing file can be thought of as a sheet resting on the drafting table in the X and Y plane, while you look down at the sheet from the Z coordinate. In looking at an actual physical 3D model resting on the same drafting table, you need to view the model from various angles and not just straight down like the plan view. Likewise, a 3D computer model needs to be viewed from various angles, such as an isometric projection or a camera perspective view.

The necessary commands for viewing in 3D are VPORTS, VPOINT (DDV-POINT), and DVIEW. The UCS command is also required in building the 3D model.

Setting Up VPORTS/VPOINTS for Multiple Views when Modeling in 3D

To work in 3D, you need to look at the model from different viewports at the same time. To create multiple views, use the VPORTS command.

`Command:VPORTS`	Issues the VPORTS command
`Save/Restore/Delete/Join/SIngle/` `?/2/<3>/4:` **3**	Specifies three viewports
`Horizontal/Vertical/Above/Below/` `Left/<Right>:` Press Enter	Specifies which viewport will be the large view

Now you have three viewports of the same image. To change the angle of the views, do either of the following:

`Command:` **DDVPOINT**	Issues the DDVPOINT command (see fig. 1.4)

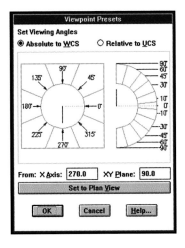

Figure 1.4

The Viewpoint Presets dialog box, displayed by issuing the DDVPOINT command.

Select the angle of the view, as well as the height, to control the viewing angle. You can also use the VPOINTS command, if you know the X, Y, Z values to enter. After a certain viewpoint is created, save the view with a name that you can remember (such as, ax-nw or ax-se). Now that the viewports are set up, use them to create lines and objects from one viewport to another.

Using DVIEW To View the Model at Various Camera Angles

After the VPORTS command is used, you can see three or four tiled viewports. The axon view created with the VPOINT command shows the model in 3D, but what if you want to show a view from a certain camera angle? To get a camera view, a perspective view has to be created. One of the powerful capabilities that today's CAD software packages offer is viewing in perspective.

Traditionally, architects were trained to construct perspective views by using station points, drafting the horizon line, establishing a distance from the object to be drawn on, drafting a plan of the object, and drafting and projecting the lines to create a perspective view of the building with some accuracy. The problem is that the perspective has to be constructed for every view, making it a painstaking process to draft and draw perspective lines. By using AutoCAD to "build" a 3D model and view the 3D model using the camera from several viewpoints, perspective view can be generated far more quickly. The perspective view is also more accurate because you have the capability to adjust the distance for the camera, the camera angle, and the lens (wide-angle or zoom). Bring this into 3D Studio, and the camera can become a motion-picture camcorder with the ability to create simple to complex animation.

The DVIEW command offers several options for viewing in isometric and perspective mode; refer to the AutoCAD Command Reference Guide and User's Guide for all the options. For traditional architectural work, the task of viewing is to mimic a person taking a picture of the 3D design with a 35 mm SLR camera. The following are the steps used to generate a perspective view, using 5'-6" as the standard camera height.

Generating a Perspective View

Command: **DVIEW**	Issues the DVIEW command
Select Objects: Select objects using window or crossing	Specifies objects to use for viewing
CAmera/TArget/Distance/POints /PAn/Zoom/TWist/CLip/Hide/Off /Undo/<eXit>: **PO**	
Enter target point<...>:**.XY** of Pick a target point (Need Z): **5'6"**	Picks target point using XY filters, prompting for Z height
Enter camera point <...>:**.XY** of Pick a camera point (Need Z): **5'6"**	
CAmera/TArget/Distance/POints /PAn/Zoom/TWist/CLip/Hide/Off /Undo/<eXit>: **D**	Changes from isometric to perspective mode
New Camera/target distance <..>: Camera to target distance	Press Enter to accept default

A perspective view of the camera, with zoom lens default at 50 mm lens, will appear on your screen.

```
CAmera/TArget/Distance/POints

/PAn/Zoom/TWist/CLip/Hide/Off

/Undo/<eXit>:Z                          Issues ZOOM command

Adjust lens length <50.000 mm>:30      Changes lens to 30 mm
```

Lens can be adjusted by typing in the lens, or by using the mouse/digitizer to adjust the lens left and right (look at the bar on top of the active viewport). Figure 1.5 shows the image with hidden lines removed.

```
CAmera/TArget/Distance/POints
/PAn/Zoom/TWist/CLip/Hide/Off
/Undo/<eXit>: H                         Issues HIDE command

Command:
```

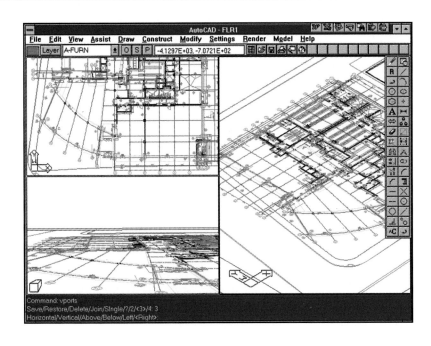

Figure 1.5
Viewports with plan, per-spective, and isometric views.

Notice that the UCS icon has changed to a perspective view of a cube, in the perspective view. Save the perspective view for quick recall.

Saving Various UCS Settings for Building Models

To work in the 3D Modeling environment, it is imperative that you understand the UCS command. When you type **UCS** at the `Command:` prompt, the following prompt appears:

`Origin/ZAxis/3Point/Entity/View/X/Y/Z/Prev/Restore/Save/Del/?<World>:`

You can review all the different options in the AutoCAD reference manuals. The procedure useful for architects would be to create and save UCS settings for the different sides of the 3D model. An example of this technique is as follows.

Take the plan view with default UCS and North pointing toward the top of the plan; South toward the bottom of the plan. To create the various UCS, there are two methods. The first method involves using DDUCSP and dialog boxes; the second involves using the command line.

Option 1

1. Issue the DDUCSP command (or choose Settings/UCS/Preset in Release 12 for Windows) to display the UCS Orientation dialog box, shown in figure 1.6.

Figure 1.6

The UCS Orientation dialog box, displayed by issuing the DDUCSP command.

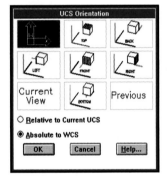

2. Select the Front box, save UCS as S-ELEV.

3. Select the Right box, save UCS as E-ELEV.

4. Select the Left box, save UCS as W-ELEV.

5. Select the Back box, save UCS as N-ELEV.

Option 2

`Command: ` **`UCS`**	Issues UCS command

`Origin/ZAxis/3Point/Entity/`
`View/X/Y/Z/Prev/Restore/Save/`
`Del/?<World>: ` **`X`**
	Selects X coordinate

`Rotate around X axis: ` **`90`**	Rotates UCS 90 degrees

`Origin/ZAxis/3Point/Entity/`
`View/X/Y/Z/Prev/Restore/Save/`
`Del/?<World>: ` **`S`**
	Saves UCS

`?/Desired UCS name: ` **`S-ELEV`**	Saves UCS for South elevation.

`Origin/ZAxis/3Point/Entity/`
`View/X/Y/Z/Prev/Restore/Save/`
`Del/?<World>: ` **`Y`**
	Selects Y coordinate

`Rotate around Y axis: ` **`90`**	Rotates UCS 90 degrees

`Origin/ZAxis/3Point/Entity/`
`View/X/Y/Z/Prev/Restore/Save/`
`Del/?<World>: ` **`S`**
	Saves UCS

`?/Desired UCS name: ` **`E-ELEV`**	Saves UCS for East elevation

Repeat the last command twice using y, rotate 90, saving UCS as N-ELEV, W-ELEV.

NOTE

You have just created a UCS that will correspond to each of the elevations of the 3D Model. To view each of the elevation views, call up the corresponding UCS (say, S-ELEV for South elevation), issue the PLAN command; zoom in to the view; and save the view (say, S-VIEW for South view).

Using the VPORTS command, you can then call up the view to see the 3D model in isometric view, elevation view, and plan view.

Exercise: Viewing in 3D

This example uses a 3D model of a house called SITE-3D.DWG that is in the ACAD (ACADWIN)/SAMPLE directory as a basis for using the preceding commands in viewing a 3D model. If you do not have this model in your AutoCAD directories, the same house is in Autodesk 3D Studio's *World Creating Toolkit* CD-ROM as NAYLOR.3DS, in the Geometry/Architex directory. Save it as a DXF file for importing to AutoCAD Release 12 or earlier, or use the 3DS file for AutoCAD Release 13.

In AutoCAD for Windows Release 12, open the SITE-3D.DWG in the \ACAD-WIN\SAMPLE directory. The model of the house with different views in paperspace will appear. Set the tilemode to 1, and enter **MS**. If the drawing is not the plan view, use the PLAN command and press Enter. You now should have a plan view of the house and the site, units in architectural, and the elevation at 50 feet (see fig. 1.7). Zoom in a little closer to see the house and the site clearly.

Figure 1.7
Plan view of house.

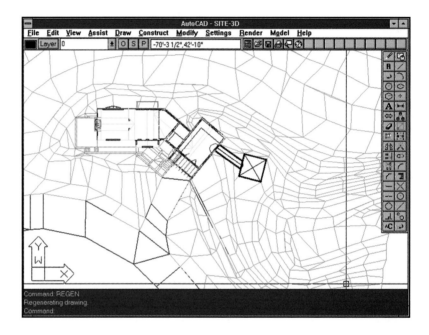

First, use the DVIEW command, to get a perspective camera view of the front of the house, and then save the view.

Getting a Perspective Camera View with DVIEW

Command: **DVIEW**   Issues the DVIEW command

Select objects: **W**   Uses the window selection

First corner: Pick top left corner   Selects the house, using window

Other corner: Pick bottom right corner

Select objects: Press Enter   Completes selection

CAmera/TArget/Distance/POints
/PAn/Zoom/Twist/Clip/Hide/Off
/Undo/<eXit>: **PO**   Selects Points option

```
Enter Target point <...>: .XY          Specifies target point
of Pick center of house               at center of house

Need Z: 5'6"                           Specifies target height

Enter Camera point <..>: .XY           See figure 1.8 for Camera Position
of Pick point to south east part

Need Z: 5'6"
```

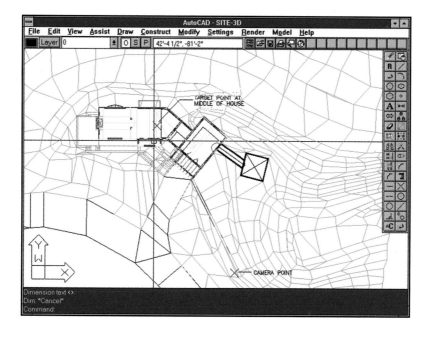

Figure 1.8
Camera and target positions for house.

```
CAmera/TArget/Distance/POints         Issues DISTANCE command to
/PAn/Zoom/Twist/Clip/Hide/Off         go to perspective mode
/Undo/<eXit>:D

New Camera/Target distance <..>:90'   Enters distance around 90'

CAmera/TArget/Distance/POints
/PAn/Zoom/Twist/Clip/Hide/Off
/Undo/<eXit>:H                        Hides lines to see image

CAmera/TArget/Distance/POints         House is zoomed too close
/PAn/Zoom/Twist/Clip/Hide/Off
/Undo/<eXit>:Z                        Issues ZOOM lens command

Adjust lens length <50 mm>: 30        Zooms lens to 30 mm

CAmera/TArget/Distance/POints
/PAn/Zoom/Twist/Clip/Hide/Off
/Undo/<eXit>:H                        Hides lines again
```

continues

```
CAmera/TArget/Distance/POints
/PAn/Zoom/Twist/Clip/Hide/Off
/Undo/<eXit>: Press Enter              Exits the DVIEW command

Command: VIEW                          Issues the VIEW command

?/Delete/Restore/Save/Window: S

View name to save: PER-1               Saves the view as PER-1
```

To see the house with the hidden lines removed, either issue the HIDE command or the SHADE command with SHADEDGE set to 2 for lines (see fig. 1.9).

Figure 1.9

Perspective view of house.

Now make multiple views of the house, one showing the plan, and another showing an isometric view. The commands to use are VPORTS, PLAN, and VPOINT (DDVPOINT).

Using the VPORTS Command

```
Command: VPORTS                        Issues the VPORTS command

Save/Restore/Delete/Join/SIngle        Selects for 3 viewports
/?/2/<3>/4: 3

Horizontal/Vertical/Above/Below
/Left/<Right>: Press Enter

Command:
```

You see three tiled viewports, all showing the same perspective view of the house. To view the plan of the house, use the PLAN command: Pick in the top left viewport to activate it (crosshairs appear when you move the cursor in the active viewport).

Using the PLAN Command

Command: **PLAN**	Issues the PLAN command
<Current UCS>/Ucs/World: Press Enter	Opens plan view of entire site
Command: **ZOOM**	Zooms in to house
All/Center/Dynamic/Extents/Left /Previous/Vmax/Window/<Scale(X/XP)>: **W**	
First Corner: Pick top right corner	
Other Corner: Pick bottom right corner	
Command: **VIEW**	Issues the VIEW command
?/Delete/Restore/Save/Window: **S**	
View name to save: **PLN-1**	Saves the plan view as PLN_1
Command:	

To see an isometric view from the southwest, click on the bottom left viewport to activate it and use one of the following options:

Using the POINT and DDVPOINT Commands

Option 1

Command: **POINT**	Issues the POINT command
Rotate/<Viewpoint> <....>: **-1,-1,1**	Point set for SW view
Regenerating drawing:	Isometric view appears
Command:	

Option 2

Command: **DDVPOINT**	Displays the Viewpoint Presets dialog box (see fig. 1.10)

continues

Figure 1.10

The Viewpoint Presets dialog box, displayed by issuing the DDVPOINT command.

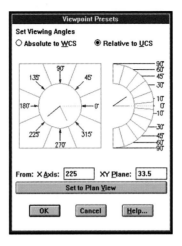

Set plan view to 225 degrees, angle to 33.5, and choose OK.

Zoom in on the house and save the view as AX-SW. Select each viewport, issue the HIDE or SHADE command to see the house with hidden line removed (see fig. 1.11).

Figure 1.11

Views of house in isometric, plan, and perspective.

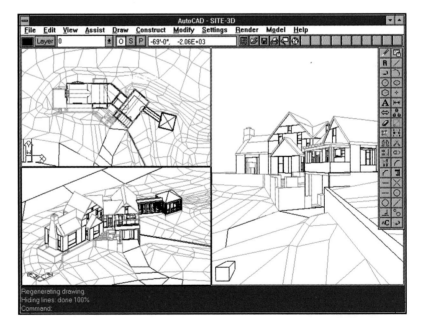

To see a Front or South elevation of the house, change the plan view of the house to the elevation view by creating a UCS oriented for the South elevation view. Activate the top left viewport by picking in the viewport with the cursor. There are two options to view this Front elevation.

The first option entails performing these steps:

1. Issue the DDUCSP command to display the UCS Orientation dialog box (refer to figure 1.6).

2. Select the Front view, choose Relative to Current UCS, and choose OK.

The second option entails performing the following exercise:

Changing the Plan View

Command: **UCS**	Issues the UCS command
Origin/ZAxis/3Point/Entity/View /X/Y/Z/Prev/Restore/Save/Del/ <World>:**X**	Rotates UCS along X axis
Rotate along x axis: **90**	
Command: **UCS**	
Origin/ZAxis/3Point/Entity/View /X/Y/Z/Prev/Restore/Save/Del/ <World>:**S**	Saves UCS
?/Desired UCS name: **S-ELV**	
Origin/ZAxis/3Point/Entity/View /X/Y/Z/Prev/Restore/Save/Del/ <World>:Press Enter	Exits UCS command
Command: **PLAN**	Issues PLAN command
<Current UCS>/Ucs/World: Press Enter	

The top left viewport will be in elevation. Zoom in closer, and save the view as S-ELEV. Use the HIDE or SHADE command to see the elevation clearly (see fig. 1.12).

Figure 1.12

Front elevation, isometric, and perspective of house.

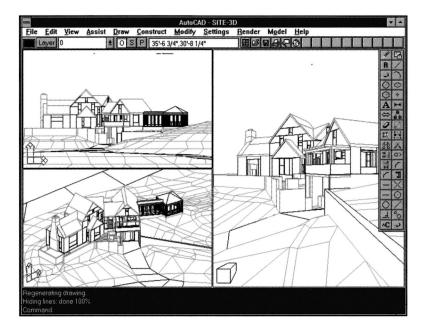

Extruding AutoCAD Lines to the Z Coordinate

One of the quickest ways to create 3D surfaces is to take the existing 2D entities and extrude them. You can create extruded lines by using the THICKNESS command to create a line with a certain height. In the current plan view with the UCS set to World, any line or pline drawn will have a height of the set thickness. The elevation command (ELEV) sets the z-coordinate value. The default for the world coordinate system is zero; any positive number will move the elevation to the corresponding height.

```
Command: ELEV
(set value for elevation) <0>: 0
```

```
Command: THICKNESS
(set value for thickness) <0>: 8'
```

Any line or polyline that you now draw in AutoCAD will have a height of 8 feet; in the current WCS plan view, the change is not evident. But if you change the view in an isometric view using the VPOINT or the DDVPOINT command, you can see the line in 3D view.

Another way is to use the CHPROP command (change properties) to change the lines from flat 2D lines to 3D lines with the certain height. A good example is to take a copy or wblock of the wall layers (say, A-WALL) from an existing 2D floor plan and change the thickness of the line from 0 to 12 feet. At the same time, change the name of the layers to a more object-oriented layer name, such as WALL01, as previously mentioned in the section on layer names.

Besides walls, a good example of using the THICKNESS command is for build-ing steel columns or wide flanges. A wide flange drawn as a closed polyline can be brought in and have the thickness changed to whatever height.

When creating the wblock of the A-wall*, remember to keep the insertion point at 0,0. A good technique is to open the wblock drawing file, issue the CHPROP command, and rename the layers in the wblock drawing before inserting and exploding in the 3D base drawing file.

Using 3D Faces To Build Surface Models

The THICKNESS command is a quick way to make the lines 3D by extruding the lines to the "z" dimension. A limitation with extruded lines is that the surfaces created are rectangular. For generating surfaces that occur in different angles or of regular and irregular three- or four-sided polygons, the 3D FACE command can be used to create a single surface.

Refer to the AutoCAD Command Reference and the User's Guide for the use and explanation of 3D faces. Faces are important for AutoCAD 3D files imported into 3D Studio because the meshes in 3D Studio are composed of faces, making up elements and objects.

For creating additional adjacent faces, you can use the 3DFACE command to continue building adjacent faces. The 3DFACE command allows you to use the third and fourth points of the last 3D face built as the first and second points of the next 3D face.

Command: **3DFACE**

First Point: Pick an endpoint (A)

Second Point: Pick an endpoint (B)

Third point: Pick an endpoint (C)

Fourth point: Pick an endpoint (D)

Third point: Pick an endpoint (E)

Fourth point: Pick an endpoint (F)

Using 3D Meshes for Complex Models

AutoCAD has a series of commands for generating 3D meshes among lines, curves, and arcs to create surface models. The commands vary depending on the type of modeling desired, such as the REVSURF command for generating a mesh along an axis; the famous wine goblet generated as a 3D mesh is a good example. Refer to the AutoCAD manuals for the use of the different types of Surface commands. Note, however, that sometimes it is easier to do the mod-eling for certain 3D mesh commands in 3D Studio using the 2D Shaper and the 3D Lofter, rather than trying to model 3D meshes entirely in AutoCAD.

Techniques in Building a 3D Model, Using Copy, Array for Repeated Components

Before you build a 3D model, think about what you will be building, how many parts the model will have, and how much detail the parts of the model need to have. One problem designers have is that the information put into a 2D drawing is usually drawn in real scale (scale 1"=1"). Architects may get carried away using the ZOOM command like a microscope to draw every detail, when in fact these details will not be visible at the viewing scale of the drawing when plotted to a hard copy. You will hear this mentioned time and again: simplify your model; do not try to build and create every thing that may not be visible in the final output. Keep the file size down to prevent large files that have an excessive number of faces that increase rendering time for images and animation in 3D Studio.

Just as in 2D drafting, the idea is to draw something correctly once. The use of the COPY, ARRAY, and 3DARRAY commands is a necessity in building 3D models.

Strategies for Building Various Components

There are several strategies for constructing a 3D model, and yet there is no one correct method of building models. A modeler may construct a part of the model differently from another modeler, yet the result looks the same. Remember, if the final result looks good, and you have achieved the appearance desired, then it's correct.

The following is a list of methods for constructing models:

◆ Extrude existing lines by changing the thickness of the lines using the CHPROP command for straight vertical elements. Create new lines with a thickness by setting the THICKNESS command to a given height of the line. Other elements include closed polyline shapes, such as a steel wide flange, which can be extruded to a given height

◆ Use the 3DFACE command to fill in holes at the top of walls or to generate irregular flat shapes (not rectangular like a line with thickness). Use 3D faces for constructing flat or sloped roofs, creating the diagonal truss members, or creating irregular four-sided shapes.

◆ To create a flat surface for a shape composed of more than four sides or with a combination of arcs and curves that can be a closed polyline entity (for example, like a city block with curbs at the corner), import the closed polyline into 3D Studio and have the closed polyline be "capped." This "mesh" can then be brought back into AutoCAD, rather than using meshes or faces to create surfaces.

- For creating mullions, use the THICKNESS command for extruding plan views. Use the MOVE command (using UCS at any of the elevations) to move objects up to the z coordinate; use the OSNAPS command. See the exercise on building the curtain wall.

- For creating glass, use 3D faces by following the corners or endpoints of the mullions; then move the glass in 1" or 2" to the correct glazing location. Note: Use simple rectangles using closed polylines for mullions. For the glazing, use a single face. (Do not try to replicate the glazing with accuracy such as insulated glass with 1" insulation, film layers, and so on unless you are creating an extreme close-up of the mullion system. From a perspective point of view, or during architectural walk-throughs, that amount of detail will never be seen.)

- Use the solid modelers for generating objects requiring unifying walls, creating openings, and using Boolean operations. Use the EXTRUDE command to generate objects by taking a closed polyline (such as a wall section) and extruding the polyline along a path to create a solid object (the Extrude feature is in AutoCAD Release 13).

- If possible, avoid using different types of 3D models when creating a model. AME models should remain as all solid models, whereas meshes should remain as surface models. Wireframes are not ideal for importing to 3D Studio's 3D editor as an object because they have no surfaces.

TIP

Always keep a notebook or a project file during the construction of your AutoCAD and 3D Studio models. Write down the steps you have taken in building certain parts, the measurements you used from certain drawing files, and the names you have given them. It's easy to try to do work by trial and error, but once you have succeeded, write it down. This will save you some time when you have to re-create an object and need to remember the steps you performed.

Exercise in 3D Modeling in AutoCAD

In this exercise, you build a curtain wall that is 16'8" wide by 32' high, with the depth of the vertical and horizontal mullions at 12", and the glazing set back 2" from the front face.

Begin AutoCAD. Set units to Architectural; accept all defaults; and create layers MULL01 and GLAZ01, making the MULL01 current.

First, you create the plan of the vertical mullions.

Creating the Plan of the Vertical Mullions

Command: **PLINE**	Issues POLYLINE command
From **0,0**,	Creating a mullion 2"×12"
Arc/Close/Halfwidth/Length/Undo /Width/<endpoint of Line>: **2,0**	
Arc/Close/Halfwidth/Length/Undo /Width/<endpoint of Line>: **2,12**	
Arc/Close/Halfwidth/Length/Undo /Width/<endpoint of Line>: **0,12**	
Arc/Close/Halfwidth/Length/Undo /Width/<endpoint of Line>: **C**	
Command: **ARRAY**	Issues the ARRAY command
Select objects: Pick mullion	
Rectangular or Polar Array (R/P)<R>: **R**	Specifies a rectangular array
Number of rows (---)<1>: Press Enter	
Number of columns (¦¦¦)<1>: **4**	To create four mullions 5'6" apart
Distance between columns (¦¦¦): **5'6"**	
Command:	
Command: **VPOINT**	Issues VPOINT command
Rotate/<Viewport><....>: **-1,-1,1**	Generates isometric view from southwest

Now, you start constructing the mullions, starting with the outside vertical mullions.

Command: **CHPROP**	Issues the CHPROP command
Select objects: Pick on the first and the last mullions	
Change what property (Color/LAyer /LType/Thickness)?: **T**	Change Thickness to 32'
New thickness <0'-0">: **32'**	

Next, you will construct the horizontal mullions. The distance between the outside vertical mullions is 16'4". The UCS will need to change for doing these mullions.

Command: **DDUCSP**	Displays the UCS Orientation dialog box

```
Select the Left box, choose Relative
to Current UCS, and choose OK
```

```
Command: THICKNESS
```
Issues THICKNESS
command

```
New value for thickness <..>: -16'4"
```
Changes thickness to -16'4"

```
Command: PLINE
from point: end of Pick endpoint of
```
Issues POLYLINE command

bottom of left outside vertical
mullion (see fig. 1.13)

```
Current line width is 0'-0"
```

```
ARc/Close/Halfwidth/Length/Undo
of line>: @2<90
```
Creating horizontal base
/Width/<Endpoint mullion

```
ARc/Close/Halfwidth/Length/Undo
/Width/<Endpoint of line>: @12<180
```

```
ARc/Close/Halfwidth/Length/Undo
/Width/<Endpoint of line>: @2<270
```

```
ARc/Close/Halfwidth/Length/Undo
/Width/<Endpoint of line>: CL
```

```
Command:
```

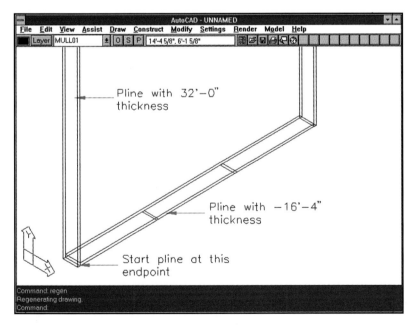

Figure 1.13

View of mullion in isometric.

Copy this horizontal mullion to the top.

```
Command: COPY
```
Issues the COPY command

continues

```
Select objects: Pick on the
horizontal mullion

<Base point of displacement>
/Multiple:@

Second point of displacement:            Copying mullion to top
 @31'-10"<90
```

For the intermediate horizontal mullions, you will copy the bottom horizontal mullion, modify the thickness, and array it vertically and horizontally. Note that the distance between vertical mullions is 5'-4".

```
Command: COPY                            Issues the COPY command

Select objects: Pick on bottom
horizontal mullion

<Base point of displacement>             Copies mullion to 3'
/Multiple:@                              above base

Second point of displacement: @3'<90

Command: CHPROP                          Issues CHPROP command

Select objects: Pick on the new
horizontal mullion

Change what property (Color/LAyer        Changes thickness to -5'4"
/LType/Thickness)?: T

New thickness <0'-0">: -5'4"
Change what property (Color/LAyer
/LType/Thickness)?:Press Enter

Command: UCS                             Issues UCS command

Origin/ZAxis/3Point/Entity/View
/X/Y/Z/Prev/Restore/Save/Del/
<World>:Press Enter                      Restores to World UCS

Command: ARRAY                           Issues the ARRAY command

Select object: Pick on last mullion

Rectangular or Polar array (R/P)<R>: R   Specifies a rectangular array

Number of rows (---)<1>:Press Enter

Number of columns (¦¦¦)<1>: 3            Indicates three mullions to
                                         be created (see fig. 1.14)

Distance between columns: (¦¦¦): 5'6"
```

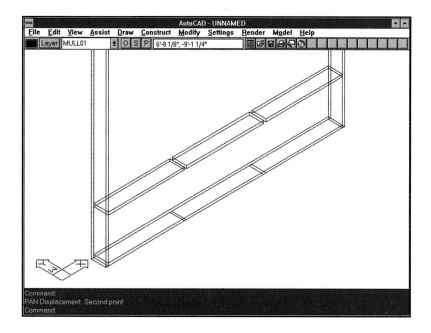

Figure 1.14

View of bottom horizontal mullions.

NOTE

Intermediate horizontal mullions created. You can issue the ZOOM command to see all the mullions.

Command: **UCS**   Issues UCS command

Origin/ZAxis/3Point/Entity/View
/X/Y/Z/Prev/Restore/Save/Del/
<World>: **P**   Restores to previous UCS

Command: **ARRAY**   Issues the ARRAY command

Select objects: Pick on the three
intermediate horizontal mullions

Rectangular or Polar array (R/P)<R>: **R**

Number of rows (---)<1>: **9**

Number of columns (¦¦¦)<3>: **1**

Unit cell or distance between
Arrays mullions to the
rows (---): **3'**

continues

Figure 1.15
Mullions arrayed vertically.

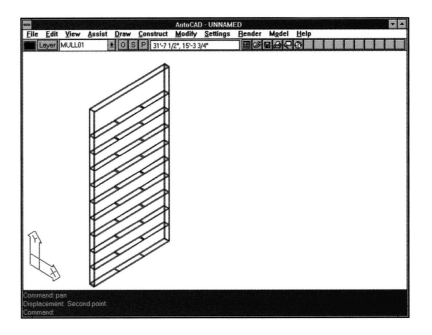

Now zoom in on the remaining vertical mullions.

```
Command: CHPROP                              Issues the CHPROP
                                             command

Select objects: Pick on the two
mullions at the base

Change what property (Color/LAyer
/LType/Thickness)?: T

New thickness <...>: 31'8"                   Changes thickness of
                                             mullions to 31'-8"
```

Let's take a look at the front elevation of the mullions, by creating two viewports, changing the UCS, and using the PLAN command.

```
Command: VPORTS                              Issues the VPORTS
                                             command

Save/Restore/Delete/Join/
SIngle/?/2/<3>/4: 2                          Creates two viewports,
                                             left and right verticals

Horizontal/Vertical/Above/
Below/Left/<Right>: R

Command: UCS                                 Issues the UCS command

Origin/ZAxis/3Point/Entity/View              Rotates along Y axis
/X/Y/Z/Prev/Restore/Save/Del/?/
```

```
<World>: Y

Rotation angle about Y-axis: 90
```

Pick in the right viewport to activate it.

```
Command: PLAN                          Issues the PLAN command
                                       (see fig. 1.16)
```

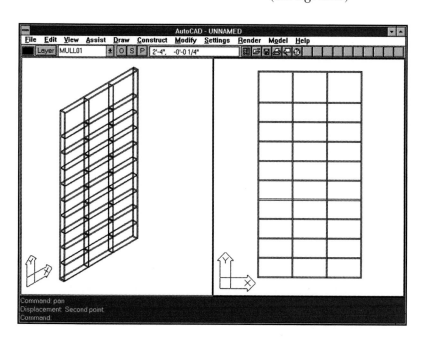

Note that the last vertical mullions are not connected to the top horizontal mullions. This is because the location of the mullion was at elevation "0," and the mullions should be resting on top of the bottom horizontal mullion.

```
Command: MOVE                          Issues the MOVE command

Select objects: Pick on the two
internal vertical mullions

Base point of displacement: @
Second point of displacement: @2<90    Moves the mullions 2" up
```

The mullions are now complete. Use the HIDE or SHADE command to see the mullions clearly.

For the glazing, you will create a 3D face. Rather than creating glazing for each frame, and thus creating 30 3D faces, the better approach would be to create a large single pane of glass for the entire curtain wall. The number of faces and vertices, which is critical when brought into 3D Studio for rendering images and animation, should be kept to a minimum to cut down on rendering time.

Pick in the left viewport (with the isometric view) to activate it.

Creating a Single Pane of Glass

Command: **VPORTS**	Issues the VPORTS command
Save/Restore/Delete/Join /SIngle/?/2/<3>/4: **SI**	Creates a single viewport
Command: Press Enter	Repeats last command
Save/Restore/Delete/Join /SIngle/?/2/<3>/4: **4**	Creates four viewports

Zoom in close to each of the four corners in the viewports (see fig. 1.17). You can use the aerial view rather than this method.

Figure 1.17

Vports set to 4 zoomed at each corner.

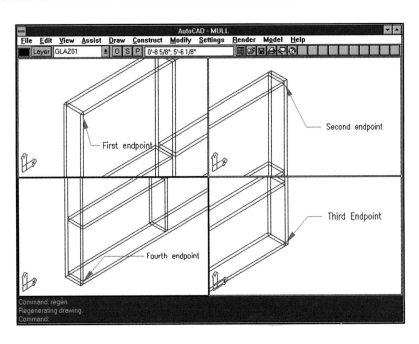

Command: **DDLMODES**	Sets current layer to GLAZ01
Command: **3DFACE**	Issues 3DFACE command

`First point:` Pick in inside
endpoint of mullion in top
left viewport (see fig. 1.17)

`Second Point:` Pick in top right
viewport, and pick on endpoint

`Third Point:` Pick in bottom right
viewport, endpoint

`Fourth Point:` Pick in bottom left
viewport, endpoint

`Third Point:` Press Enter

Now, you move the glazing
2" inward>.

`Command:` **UCS**	Issues the UCS command
`Origin/ZAxis/3Point/Entity/View` `/X/Y/Z/Prev/Restore/Save/Del/?/` `<World>:` **P**	Restores previous UCS
`Command:` **MOVE**	Issues the MOVE command

`Select objects:` Pick on glazing

`Base point of displacement:` **@**

`Second point of displacement:` **@ 2"<180**

Be sure that the OSNAP or DDOSNAP command is set to none when moving a
very small distance.

The curtain wall is now complete and is ready for exporting to 3D Studio by
the DXFOUT or 3DSOUT command. Issue the HIDE or SHADE command for a
clearer view.

Preparation of 3D Model for 3D Studio /DXFOUT, 3DSOUT

In AutoCAD releases prior to R13, use the DXFOUT command for bringing the
AutoCAD 3D models into 3D Studio. The preferred method is to use the
Binary option to reduce the file size and save a DXF file to a higher precision.
Blocks and xrefs can also be imported into 3D Studio using the Binary option.
Use the entities options if only a certain object or objects need to be imported
into 3D Studio.

The Filmroll option is another file format that can be merged into 3D Studio
from AutoCAD. The filmroll file, however, is unsuitable if there are more than
256 objects because this can load in only by the color of the lines; AutoCAD
is limited to 256 colors. This option has been discontinued in AutoCAD
Release 13.

AutoCAD Release 13 has a 3DSOUT feature that creates 3DS files for importing into 3D Studio. Enter **3DSOUT** at the Command: prompt (or pull down File/Export/ and select .3DS Files under type of files). Upon selecting the objects, the dialog box appears allowing control of shading and degrees of angle. 3DSOUT converts saved AutoCAD named views into 3D Cameras and Autovision lights to the nearest equivalent 3D Studio lights (see fig. 1.18).

Figure 1.18

3DSOUT dialog box in AutoCAD Release 13.

Tips for Importing Files from AutoCAD

The following are tips for importing files from AutoCAD to 3D Studio from Ted Boardman, an Autodesk multimedia educational training specialist who teaches 3D Studio at the Autodesk Training Center in Boston at Autodesk University. He also is currently president of the New England 3D Studio Users Group.

- ◆ Draw accurately. Always use OSNAPS to ensure vertices are as good as possible.

- ◆ Use Release 12's region Modeler to create complex surfaces from existing 2D plans; use ALIGN to assemble into a 3D model.

- ◆ Use high enough Surftab 1 and Surftab 2 settings to get a good model, but don't overdo it.

- ◆ Adjust DXF-ARC-DEGREES in the 3DS.SET file to get smooth arcs from AutoCAD R12.

- ◆ Use the Binary option of DXFOUT for the best results and for smaller DXF files.

- ◆ Set Weld Vertices and Unify Normals off in the Loading DXF File dialog box. Weld the vertices once in 3D Studio.

- ◆ Explode copies of AME models down to the 3DFACE level before using DXFOUT.

3D Modeling in 3D Studio

3D Studio is powerful modeling, rendering, and animation software. Its main advantage is its capability to be run on the PC instead of using an expensive workstation, plus the low price in comparison to the high-end computer graphics package. For most AutoCAD modelers, 3D Studio has been used mainly for rendering photorealistic computer images and creating 3D computer animation. Some 3D AutoCAD modelers (myself included) have not used the 2D Shaper and 3D Lofter for modeling, relying instead on the 3D Editor for camera and lighting; adding materials to the objects from the Materials Editor; and using the Keyframer for creating animation. AutoCAD is a more precise drafting and modeling tool; dimensions drawn and built in AutoCAD have a greater degree of precision, down to a fraction of an inch or a number of places past the decimal point. 3D Studio, as a modeler, cannot meet the precision of AutoCAD; first and foremost, 3D Studio is more of a graphic artists tool, where "models" do not have to conform to precise units. (3D Studio MAX, judging from the preview, seems to promise more precise control.) But the combination of using AutoCAD to create a precise model and bringing that model into 3D Studio for animation and materials, is an ideal medium. Furthermore, the use of 3D Studio for modeling can take advantage of shapes and polylines from AutoCAD for creating complicated shapes.

Learning basic 3D Studio is relatively simple by using the 3D Studio tutorials. The difficulty of mastering 3D Studio depends on the goals you want to achieve—for example, realistic photographic type images or highly sophisticated computer animation. Trying to create projects such as the award-winning animation featured in the computer magazines or in Autodesk's animation CD-ROM or videos can be overwhelming. You need to realize that effective animation works as long as the message you are trying to convey to your audience, such as the quality of their proposed design, is delivered effectively.

Overview of 3D Studio's Five Modules

3D Studio Release 4 is divided into five parts, called *modules*; each of which performs a different function in creating 3D models, adding materials, and rendering stills and animation. The five modules are as follows:

◆ **2D Shaper.** In this module, you can create 2D shapes and lines for extrusion and lofting into 3D objects. AutoCAD files of 2D closed polylines and 2D lines or arcs can be brought in to the 2D Shaper for modeling 3D objects, as well as creating and modifying paths for animation.

◆ **3D Lofter.** Here you can take the shapes built in the 2D Shaper and loft or extrude them into 3D objects. Complex shapes can be created by use of the many controls available and can be brought into the 3D Editor.

- ◆ **3D Editor.** This is the module that appears when 3D Studio is first started. In this main module, you can create 3D objects, assign materials, set up lights and cameras, and render still images. For importing AutoCAD files (DXF, FLM, or 3DS in Release 13), this is the module you use to bring in the AutoCAD 3D model.

- ◆ **Keyframer.** This is the animation center of 3D Studio. Here you can move objects, cameras, and lights, and create animation. The name comes from the term that traditional animation used in films; chief animators develop a series of key frames for scenes.

- ◆ **Materials Editor.** This module assigns and creates "realistic" materials. Materials provided by 3D Studio can be used for assigning to the objects, but in the Materials Editor you can create "new materials" by using the various features of the module and the various "textures" on CD-ROMs or scanned images for "mapping" materials.

Coordination between AutoCAD and 3D Studio

The beauty of using AutoCAD and 3D Studio is the capability to import AutoCAD files into 3D Studio, and they both have the same coordinate systems (the World Coordinate System 0,0,0 in AutoCAD equals the same coordinate system in 3D Studio). 3D Studio 3DS models exported to AutoCAD can be modified constantly by performing the revisions in AutoCAD using the base AutoCAD 3D model and bringing in the revised object into 3D Studio. The object can then replace some existing objects at the exact same location. Likewise, 3D Studio models can be brought back into AutoCAD. Keep in mind that you must set up the units the same for both AutoCAD (Command: units) and 3D Studio (in the 3D Editor, pull down the Views menu under Unit Setup). It would be beneficial for AutoCAD users to change the settings for the X, Y, and Z coordinates in the 3DS.SET file to correspond to AutoCAD's World Coordinate System.

What Can and Cannot Be Imported from AutoCAD into 3D Studio

Certain issues need to be addressed for what can be imported from AutoCAD to 3D Studio. The following is an illustration of lines, faces, and objects created in AutoCAD (see fig. 1.19).

The technical aspects of the conversion are as follows:

- ◆ Closed and flat 2D polylines, 3D polylines, and circles import as a coplanar mesh determined by their perimeter. Polyline arc segments and circles are segmented.

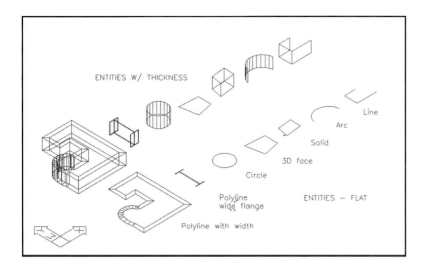

Figure 1.19
Entities in AutoCAD for import to 3D Studio.

◆ 3D Faces import as rectilinear meshes in respect to the edge visibility assigned to them in AutoCAD.

◆ Solids and traces import as rectilinear meshes having an invisible diagonal edge.

◆ Lines, arcs, and open 2D polylines with thickness import as extruded meshes. The entity appears as in AutoCAD except that it now has top and bottom vertices where before it had only one vertex level and a thickness property. The diagonal edge connecting the vertices is always invisible. Polyline arc segments and circles are segmented.

◆ Closed 2D polylines and circles with thickness import as extruded meshes with their tops and bottoms capped as coplanar meshes. Polyline arc segments and circles are segmented.

◆ Traces and solids with thickness properties are extruded and capped top and bottom.

◆ 2D polylines with width properties, closed or open, are imported with their widths defining the extents of the mesh. If the polyline has a thickness in addition to the width property, it is widened and extruded along its length.

◆ Blocks that have the entity previously listed import their entities as described. Blocks created by using the HATCH command are always composed of separate line segments, so that they cannot be imported in the 3D Editor. Such entities could, however, be brought into the Shaper and the Lofter.

AutoCAD DXF/3DS Models Loaded/Merged into 3D Studio

When you load or merge a DXF file from AutoCAD Release 12 or earlier into 3D Studio, a dialog box appears providing you with options regarding how you want your DXF file to be imported.

The first line describes what you want to derive objects from, giving you the option to derive objects by layer, color, or entity. If you used the layering convention of naming the 3D objects in AutoCAD by the appropriate layer names, then the Layer option is the correct choice. Deriving objects by color corresponds to the color of the layers. If every object has been assigned by color in AutoCAD, then the color option is viable—but with the limitation of 256 colors in AutoCAD. Another disadvantage would be that the objects would need to be renamed. The Entity option would make every AutoCAD entity into a separate object starting with the name Entity01.

Regarding the other options, Weld Vertices should be turned off to provide you with the option to weld vertices later during the modeling stage. Unify Normals is typically set to Yes, as is Autosmooth. Refer to the AutoDesk 3D Studio manual (or NRP's *Inside 3D Studio*) for a more complete description of these controls.

Importing 3DS models for AutoCAD Release 13 eliminates the need for the DXF dialog box in 3D Studio because the 3DSOUT command in AutoCAD Release 13 allows you to determine how the 3DS file will be created (by layer, color, welding vertices, and so on).

Where Are the Curves and Arcs? Segmentation in 3D Studio

Curved elements, such as arcs and splined polylines in AutoCAD, become segmented when imported into 3D Studio. Controls in 3D Studio allow for more segmentation, or using the DXF3DS.EXE can convert DXF files with more control before importing into 3D Studio. One effective way of importing curves from AutoCAD is to not use arcs at all, but rather use a straight line segments. Figures 1.19 and 1.20 show objects—drawn in AutoCAD as arcs, curves, and circles—become a series of straight line segments connected together when imported into 3D Studio.

Use of Polygons, Segmented Faces in AutoCAD

The following illustrates the strategies for creating a curved roof with a radius of 300 feet.

1. Use the ARC command to create an arc with a radius of 300'.

2. Using the DIVIDE command, set pdmode to something besides 0. Divide arc to 12.

3. Use the COPY command.

4. Use the 3DFACE command and osnap to endpoint and node.

Use of DXF3DS.EXE for Precise Curve/Arc Control

DXF3DS, discussed in detail in *Inside 3D Studio*, is a program from the Yost Group developed for more control in converting DXF files from AutoCAD to 3DS files. You may have to check in the 3D Studio Compuserve Forum to download the executable. Previous versions were called DXF3DSI.EXE or DXF3DSW.EXE (for Intel or Weitek math coprocessors).

Where Are the Models? Flipping Faces/Normals Strategies

DXF files loaded or merged into 3D Studio usually are brought in with the faces correct. But most of the time, you will notice that faces, elements, or objects that are visible in the 3D Studio 3D Editor may not appear when rendered. You can verify whether the faces are flipped correctly by going to the Display/Geometry/Backface to see which faces need to be flipped. To correct the invisible faces, you can choose Surfaces/Normals/Face Flip, or Object Flip. This may be a time-consuming procedure if you had several faces that need to be flipped, but by using the Select option and hiding other objects, and flipping the selected objects, this may cut down on the time. Using the 3DSOUT command in AutoCAD Release 13, the problem of flipped faces may be minimized. If you don't have the time to correct the faces for rendering a still image, you can render using the forced two-sided options (this may increase rendering time depending on the size of the 3DS file.

Exporting Files from 3D Studio to AutoCAD

3D Studio provides for saving files as a DXF for exporting to AutoCAD (3DS file for Release 13). Upon saving the file, 3D Studio prompts you to save to layers By Object, By Material, or 1 Layer or to Cancel. Choosing By Object exports each object as a layer with the name of the object and may be closely tied to the layering setup in AutoCAD. Choosing By Material creates a single entity of all faces made of the same material. Choosing 1 Layer creates an entire model as one entity on one layer.

Notice that the 3D model brought from AutoCAD to 3D Studio and then taken back to AutoCAD through the DXF process will vary greatly from the original AutoCAD model. The DXF models from 3D Studio will be polyface meshes. AutoCAD commands such as STRETCH, ROTATE, SCALE, and MOVE work on these polyface meshes, but you cannot edit these using the PEDIT command. Exploding these polyface meshes will break it up into individual 3D faces.

Strategies of Using AutoCAD and 3D Studio for 3D Modeling

◆ Use AutoCAD to create 3D models with precise units and exact positions, creating quick simple geometry.

◆ Use 3D Studio to create complex objects that are difficult in straight AutoCAD, using AutoCAD for creating shapes and paths for lofting complex objects.

◆ Import objects back and forth between AutoCAD and 3D Studio, using the AutoCAD model as a base for coordinating with existing site plans and floor plans, as a repository of 3D objects for importing into 3D Studio, and as a place to build additional objects for refined detail and correct placement.

◆ Use 3D Studio for making complex objects to use as preliminary design tools that have been modified by Boolean operation, deform, twisted, morphed, and curved, which would be difficult in AutoCAD; and import them into AutoCAD to get more precise dimensioning to make the model a more buildable "reality."

Exercise: Building the Gateway Arch Using AutoCAD and 3D Studio

The Gateway Arch, in St. Louis, Missouri was designed by Eero Saarinen, a Finnish architect who won the competition for a memorial commemorating President Thomas Jefferson's expansion of the West in making the Louisiana Purchase part of the United States of America. Saarinen won the international competition in the 1947 at age 37 but died in the fall of 1961, a few months before construction began on the Gateway Arch, which was completed in 1964.

The Gateway Arch is a good example of architecture that cannot simply be designed using straight lines, due to the cantenary arch shape, with stainless steel triangular shapes that vary in size from the two bases to the keystone at the top. The design was done before the use of computers for CAD as we know it today. Saarinen, a sculptor of buildings, did several buildings that simply cannot be drawn by straight lines, but were rather expressive 3D sculptures, such as his TWA terminal at John F. Kennedy International Airport, the Ingalls Hockey Rink at Yale University, and the airport terminal at Dulles International Airport outside Washington, D.C.

In this exercise, you use AutoCAD to generate the triangular shapes of the bases and the keystone, and the path in the shape of the cantenary arch. You then import these models into 3D Studio to create the arch, and the import it back into AutoCAD to see the results.

In AutoCAD, set the units to architectural units, fractions to 1/8", limits to 1000',1000'.

You create layers named path and arch, and make path active.

Coordinating between AutoCAD and 3D Studio

Command: **PLINE**	Issues the POLYLINE command
From point: **630',0"**	Draws a polyline arc as path, starting point
Current line-width is 0",0"	
Arc/Close/Halfwidth/Length/Undo /Width/<Endpoint of Line>: **A**	
Angle/CEnter/CLose/Direction/ Halfwidth/Line/Radius/Second Pt./ Undo/Width/<Endpoint of arc>: **S**	Second point of arc
Second Point: **601'8",234'**	
End Point: **518',454'**	Endpoint of first arc
Angle/CEnter/CLose/Direction/ Halfwidth/Line/Radius/Second Pt./ Undo/Width/<Endpoint of arc>: **S**	Continue to second arc
Second Point: **474'5,524'11**	Second point
End Point: **418',586'6"**	Endpoint of second arc
Angle/CEnter/CLose/Direction/ Halfwidth/Line/Radius/Second Pt./ Undo/Width/<Endpoint of arc>: **S**	Continue to third arc
Second Point: **370'9,617'3**	Second point
End Point: **315',630'**	Endpoint of third arc
Angle/CEnter/CLose/Direction/ Halfwidth/Line/Radius/Second Pt./Undo/Width/<Endpoint of arc>:Press Enter	Exits PLINE command

continues

```
Command:
```

You have just drawn half of the path for the arch. Next, you mirror the arch and join the arches together.

`Command: `**`MIRROR`**	Issues the MIRROR command
`First point of mirror line: `**`315',630'`**	Top point of the arch
`Second Point: `Set Ortho on, move cursor down vertically, and pick a point	
`Delete old objects? <N>: `**`N`**	
`Command: `**`PEDIT`**	Issues the POLYLINE EDIT	command
`Select polyline: `Pick an arc	

`Close/Join/Width/Edit vertex/Fit/`
`Spline/Decurve/LType gen/`
`Undo/eXit <X>: `**`J`**
	Joins the pline arcs

`Select object: `Pick an arc	
`Select object: `Pick the other arc	
`Select Object: `Press Enter	
`3 segments added to polyline`	Arcs have been joined

`Close/Join/Width/Edit vertex/Fit/`
`Spline/Decurve/LType gen/Undo`
`/eXit <X>: `Press Enter
	Exits PEDIT

```
Command:
```

Next, you draw two triangular sections for the base and the keystone of the arch. Set layer to "arch."

`Command: `**`POLYGON`**	Issues POLYGON command
`Number of sides <4>: `**`3`**	Three-sided equilateral triangle
`Edge/<center of polygon>: `Pick a point	
`Inscribed in circle/Circumscribed` `about circle (I/C)<C>: `**`I`**	Chooses Inscribed in circle
`Radius of circle: `**`24'`**	

Repeat the preceding steps for radius of 12 feet. See figure 1.20 for the image in AutoCAD.

You are now ready to import a DXF file to 3D Studio. Issue the DXFOUT command, select the path and the two triangles using entities, and give it the name ARCH.DXF (save this file in your C:\ACAD or ACADWIN, or C:\R13 directory). Save your ACAD file if you want and exit AutoCAD.

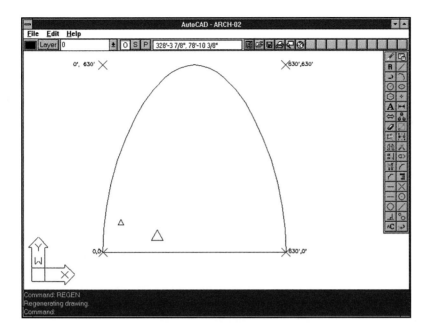

Figure 1.20
AutoCAD image of the arc path and the two triangles.

TIP

Make sure that you have set the DXF-ARC-DEGREES from 30 to about 5 in the 3DS.SET file, for better importing of arcs.

1. Start up 3D Studio, go to the 2D Shaper (choose Program/2D Shaper or press the F1 key), and choose Views/Unit Setup. Set to Architectural Units, 1/8" fractions, and choose OK.

2. Load or merge the ARCH.DXF file, use the defaults in the dialog box for now, and the path and the two triangles should appear.

Notice that there are six vertices on the path; each vertex represents the start and end of each single arc created in AutoCAD. The path could use more vertices to allow for smoother segmentation.

3. Choose Modify/Segment/Refine, and add six vertices roughly equally spaced on the first base arc; add two vertices on the middle arc; and one vertex on the top arc. Repeat for the mirror image of the arcs (see fig. 1.21).

4. Choose Shapes/Assign and select the large triangle. Choose Shapes/Check, and you should see Shapes OK, Vertices 3.

5. Press the F2 key to go to the 3D Lofter, and choose Shape/Get/Shaper. The large triangle should appear on the bottom of the path. Choose Shapes/Center, to center the triangle to the path.

Figure 1.21

The arcs and the triangles in the 2D Shaper.

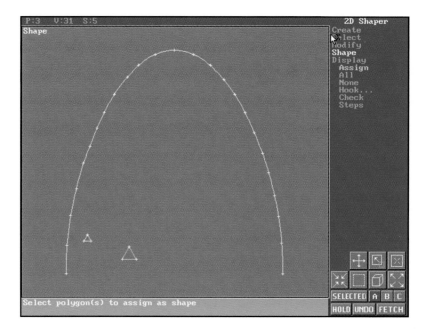

6. Press the F1 key to return to the 2D Shaper, pick on the large triangle to unassign it, and pick on the path. Press the F2 key and choose Path/Get/Shaper. Select OK when the warning appears, and the path should be replaced by the arch.

7. Zoom in on the triangle and choose Shapes/Rotate. Rotate the triangle so that the corner is pointed inward to the arch. Next, choose Shapes/Pick and pick on the top of the arch.

8. Press the F1 key, pick on the path to unassign it, and pick on the smaller triangle. Press the F2 key, choose Shapes/Get/Shaper, and the small triangle appears at the top. Again, choose Shapes/Rotate to rotate the triangle so that the edge points inward to the arch.

9. Choose Shapes/Pick and pick on the end of the path without the first large triangle. Press the F1 key, unassign the small triangle, pick on the large triangle, and press the F2 key. Choose Get/Shapes/Shaper. Rotate the triangle (see fig. 1.22).

10. You are now ready to build the arch. Choose Objects/Preview. In the dialog box, set Tween on and notice that the screen shows a preview of how the triangles are going to be lofted. Next, choose Objects/Make, set Tween and Counter on, set values to high, and click on create. Figure 1.23 shows the dialog box.

Go to the 3D Editor to see the Gateway Arch created (see fig. 1.24).

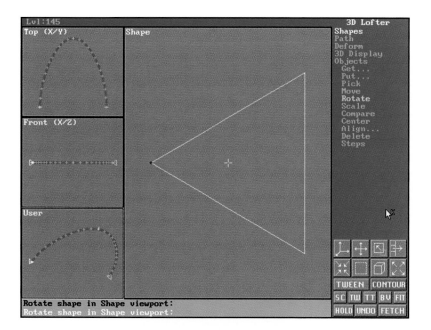

Figure 1.22
The path and the triangles in the 3D Lofter.

Figure 1.23
The Object Lofting Controls dialog box.

Depending on your X, Y, Z setup in 3D Studio, you might need to rotate the entire arch 90 degrees to correspond with the correct Top, Front, Left, and Right viewports.

11. Use the Objects/Rotate command, setting the axis at one end of the Arch, and rotate it upright accordingly. Create a base for the Arch using the Create/ Box command; add lights and cameras (see fig. 1.25).

12. Choose Renderer/Setup/Background and choose a sky background from the maps directory. Choose Renderer/Render View, activate the Camera viewport, and render the image (see fig. 1.26).

Figure 1.24

*The Gateway Arch in the
3D Editor.*

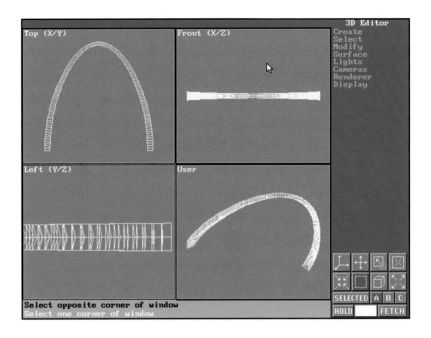

Figure 1.25

*Camera, lights, and a base
for the arch.*

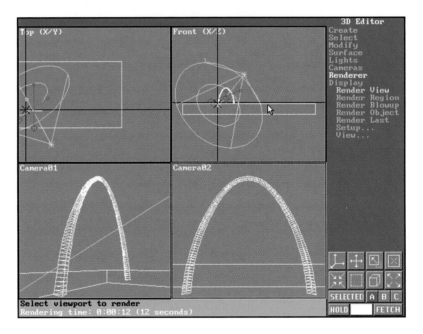

Save as a DXF file (3DS for AutoCAD Release 13) by object, and import this into AutoCAD. The model can now be used as part of the model building required in AutoCAD and for importing back into 3D Studio (see fig. 1.27).

Figure 1.26
Rendering of the Gateway Arch.

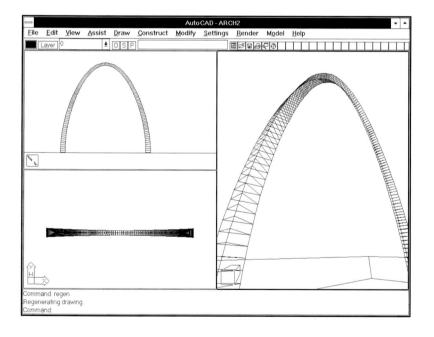

Figure 1.27
Arch imported into AutoCAD from 3D Studio.

NOTE

Readers interested in precise architectural modeling in 3D Studio using AutoCAD shapes should refer to Phillip Miller's chapter titled "Precise Lofting with AutoCAD Shapes and Paths" in the book *3D Studio Special Effects* by New Riders Publishing.

Summary

This chapter illustrates the use of basic 3D modeling and explores how to "visualize" in 3D. The chapter also discusses the use of AutoCAD for precise dimensioning in modeling, and the powerful modeling capabilities of 3D Studio, which many AutoCAD 3D modelers have not yet tapped. CAD users who have the ability to think and "visualize" in 3D will be more successful in the transition from 2D to 3D. A good tip is to study some 3D models in Autodesk's samples in both AutoCAD and 3D Studio. Examine these samples; take them apart (make a copy first) and see how the models, such as the space shuttle or the '57 Chevy BelAir, are built. Have patience in learning and mastering the techniques, and the results will be worth it.

Textures and Materials

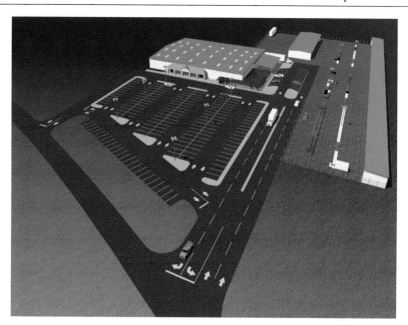

by Brandon Bartlett
Albertville, Alabama

Author Bio

Brandon Bartlett has been using AutoCAD and related graphics software for 10 years. He began his career as an "ink on vellum" draftsman working in the afternoons after high school. His experience includes working as a draftsman, designer (architectural and construction engineering), project manager, CAD integrator, and programmer.

He now works with his father's business, Bartlett Drafting and Design, offering freelance drafting and CAD consulting services to architects, engineers, and industry all over the Southeastern United States. He has worked on projects for clients as far away as the Middle East, Europe, the Caribbean, and Southeast Asia. He is also the founding partner of DesignTec, a computer graphics and animation firm specializing in architectural visualization and industrial simulations.

Brandon's CompuServe address is 74644,3053; he can also be reached via the Internet at bartlett@airnet.net.

Chapter Overview

The popularity of computer-generated renderings continues to rise among architects and building designers. Traditional methods of presentation are far from gone, but many designers now realize the benefits of 3D modeling and rendering on the computer. One of the factors that sets computer-generated artwork apart from, say, traditional ink renderings, is the capability to apply highly realistic color textures to 3D objects created on the computer. Applied correctly and with care, quality textures and materials can enhance even simple 3D models to create a realistic and believable scene.

This chapter looks at ways to use textures and materials to add that extra tinge of realism to your scene, so that you are better equipped to convey your vision of the design to your audience.

Architectural Textures

The eye is demanding, and so are clients. The more computer graphics are used in the motion picture industry and television, the more realism clients and the public expect when they see other forms of computer art and presentations, including architectural renderings. Using high-quality textures for architectural visualization is a must, therefore, to achieve the realism everyone expects and wants.

3D Studio ships with a nice selection of texture bitmaps and materials, accessible in the Materials Editor by loading the 3DS.MLI materials library. For detailed architectural renderings, however, the bitmaps and materials included with 3D Studio might not always be enough. Considering the enormous diversity of construction materials available to the designer in today's market, the use of third-party texture libraries and the ability to scan and create your own textures is almost indispensable.

NOTE

> **Although not described in detail in this chapter, 3D Studio's SXP (Solid Pattern External Process) plug-ins provide an additional method of applying materials. SXPs are based not on bitmaps, but on programmed equations, which generate a 3D pattern that is cast through the mesh object rather than simply being applied to the mesh's surface. Therefore, SXPs do not require mapping coordinates. The pattern generated can be static, or can be animated over time and can be used in place of any map or mask except reflections. Included in the 3D Studio installation are several sample SXPs. Descriptions of the included plug-ins, as well as instructions for their use, can be found in the *Advanced User Guide* manual that came with your copy of 3D Studio.**

Third-Party Texture Libraries

Several companies have compiled and published texture libraries, usually on CD-ROM. Several of these libraries are well suited for use on architectural models. These libraries usually include tileable bitmapped images of such things as stone, masonry, grass, stucco, various roofing materials, wood, and fabrics. Also helpful, they usually contain collections of various images that can serve as props in a scene, such as pictures of people in various poses, vehicles, trees, shrubs, animals, background scenes, and clouds.

The *Blocks and Materials CD-ROM* from Ketiv Technologies, Inc., and Modern Medium, Inc., was produced and originally bundled with Ketiv's ARCHT add-on program for Autodesk's AutoCAD software. It contains more than 600 pre-built, ready-to-render 3D objects common to architectural renderings. More relevant to this discussion, it also sports a well-arranged architecturally oriented library that contains more than 400 bitmapped textures in 24-bit TGA and 8-bit GIF formats. You can purchase the *Blocks and Materials CD-ROM* separately from Ketiv Technologies, Inc., for around $200.

Pixar has produced a fine set of photographic textures called *Pixar One Twenty Eight*. As the name suggests, it contains 128 high-quality tileable bitmaps of such things as brick, fences, metals, roofs, sidings, walls, wood, and more. They come in 512×512×24 bit and 128×128×8 bit TIFF format and tile seamlessly. You can purchase the single CD-ROM for about $170.

Some other notable texture and material libraries are *ImageCELS* by Imagetecs, Autodesk's own *Texture Universe*, *Wraptures One and Two* from Form and Function, and various collections from Visual Software and The Valis Group. These libraries often range in price from $99 to $250.

If you can't find what you need in the CD-ROM libraries, you can try some of the online sources available. Online services, such as CompuServe and America Online, offer forums and areas in which popular 3D software packages are supported and users can share models and textures. 3D Studio users can use the Autodesk Multimedia Forums on CompuServe.

The global Internet virtually teems with sites, both corporate and personal, at which you can find hundreds, and sometimes thousands, of images and textures. 3D artists also gather on various bulletin board systems, such as the Rendering Plant BBS, to share, trade, and sell 3D models and textures.

 NOTE

If you don't know where to find some of these online sources for textures, here are a few starting points. On CompuServe, GO AMMEDIA and GO ASHOWCASE take you to the Autodesk Multimedia Forums. On the Internet, the following URLs (Uniform Resource Locators) can get you started:

```
ftp://avalon.viewpoint.com/pub/textures

http://sunserver1.rz.uni-duesseldorf.de/~pannozzo/3ds.html
```

You can contact the Rendering Plant BBS as follows:

(816) 525-8362	v.34 modems
(816) 525-5614	v.32 modems
(816) 525-0103	VOX
(816) 525-1594	FAX

Scan and Make Your Own Textures

If you still can't find what you need, you need to create your own custom textures. Many prefer this method for architectural visualization, because it gives you more complete control over the images you use.

You can get good pictures into digital format for use with your computer software in several ways. Digital cameras, which use a digital storage device such as a small hard drive rather than film for holding the image, are continuing to improve in both image quality and affordability. On the other hand, many film processing companies are beginning to offer the service of transferring images from 35mm film to CD-ROM. You can get a roll of 35mm film printed to CD-ROM for as little as $19.95, and you can buy the software necessary to view, edit, and save these images to your hard drive for as low as $35.

If you have a good color scanner, preferably a flatbed scanner for best results, you can scan your own images—easily the most flexible method, because you can scan anything, from carpet and wallpaper swatches to brick and marble tile. If you already know the finishes for the structure you're planning to model and render, having your own scanner enables you to create custom textures from the real-world materials to be used in the actual construction.

Use your imagination. With a little creativity and a scanner, you can create textures for just about anything you need.

NOTE

I once needed to create the effect of old faded paper, the kind of weathered and rough edged paper that a treasure map might be on. I couldn't find anything in my texture libraries that worked. So, half seriously, I took a sheet of copier paper and wadded it up tightly several times. I folded the paper out flat and laid it on the scanner. Voilá, I had a wrinkled image that I could use both as a texture map and as a bump map to create exactly the effect I desired.

Bump Mapping

Bump mapping enables you to add 3D surface features to models without having to create or edit 3D geometry. Bump mapping doesn't affect the original mesh object. Rather, when you render the scene, it simulates the lighting effect that produces highlights and shadows across an irregular surface.

Bump mapping is based on the luminance value, or brightness, of each pixel in the bump map image. Black being *no bump*, white being *fully bumped out*, or raised from the original surface, and the 254 different luminance values in between creating an increasingly *bumped* effect as they approach white.

Because bump mapping is based only on the luminance value of each pixel, using color bitmaps as bump maps can be confusing. The colors you see in a true color image are based on three different values—hue, luminance, and saturation (commonly referred to as the HLS color model)—and 3D Studio ignores all but the luminance, or intensity, when creating a bump map. Visually discerning the luminance values of particular areas or pixels in a color image can be difficult, so results can be very unpredictable when you use a color image in 3D Studio as a bump map.

TIP

If you want to see the effect a color image would have as a bump map, load the image into an image editing or paint program and convert it to a 256 grayscale image. This will enable you to clearly see the changes in luminance across the image.

Bump mapping techniques can be used to quickly and effectively add detail where the construction materials being simulated in the architectural rendering have repetitive surface features, such as ribbed metal panels, brick, masonry, and tile, to name a few. The following two sections discuss simple ways to enhance the look of ribbed metal panels and concrete block walls without additional modeling.

Simulating Ribbed Metal Panels

Ribbed metal panels and standing seam metal roof systems have become increasingly popular wall and roof finishes in recent decades. Hence, it's quite likely that you will need to simulate this construction material in an architectural rendering at some point.

To create this effect by modeling each rib, not only would consume considerable time, but also would weigh down your model with too many unnecessary faces and vertices and slow down rendering times. Using a bump map to simulate the ribs, on the other hand, would solve all of that.

First, you need a good image for the bump map. You can start by following these steps:

1. Create a 256 grayscale image in an image editing or paint program.

2. Make the entire image completely black.

3. Within that image, create a vertical gradient between black and white, or no luminance and full luminance.

4. Mirror that gradient so that the two resultant gradients are adjacent, with the color white in the middle, fading away in both horizontal directions back to black.

After you finish, you should end up with an image that looks something like figure 2.1. The image's resolution is not necessarily important. Just remember that you do not want the image so large that it eats up RAM at rendering time or so small that there are too few pixels to create a smooth gradient. The resolution of figure 2.1 is 512×512 pixels, which is typical in many texture libraries.

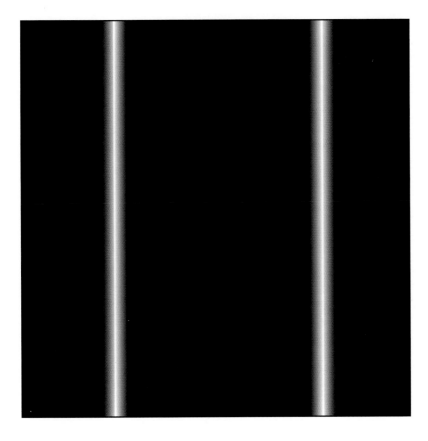

Figure 2.1

A bitmap image suitable for use as a bump map to simulate ribbed metal panels. The gradient transition from black (no bump) to white (fully bumped) and back to black again creates the effect of the sloping sides of the rib in the metal panel.

An image similar to figure 2.1 should be sufficient for simulating just about any ribbed metal panel or standing seam metal panel you might need. Although many manufacturers provide more complex profiles for their metal panels, you probably won't ever need to view the panels that closely, unless the panels themselves are the focus of the scene.

Figure 2.2 is a closeup of a metal roof modeled using the previously described method. The roof itself is nothing more than a 2D set of faces with a red metal material applied along with the bump map in figure 2.1.

Figure 2.2

The ribbed metal roof effect created using a simple bump map.

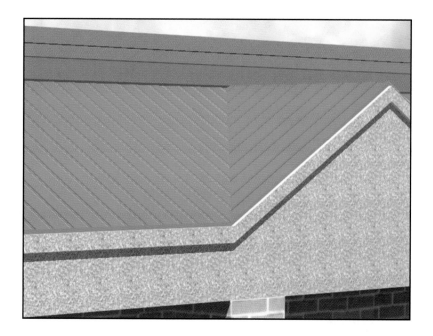

Enhancing Masonry and Tile Textures

The various forms of masonry units and tile are very common construction materials. Bump mapping can add an extra touch of realism to masonry and tile textures. For instance, take a look at figure 2.3.

The brick column shown in figure 2.3 looks nice, but can look even better if you use a simple bump map. The bump map needs to overlay the brick texture accurately, or the rendered results will be less than gratifying. All mapping types (with the exception of SXPs) use the same mapping coordinates for any particular object, so the easiest thing to do is to base the bump map on the brick bitmap itself.

In the following exercise, you use the brick texture bitmap as the bump map to simulate the 3D surface features of a real brick column with mortar joints.

Figure 2.3

A brick column rendered with a simple brick texture.

1. Load the brick bitmap into an image editing program.

2. Convert the image to grayscale. This helps you see the effect the bitmap has when used as the bump map.

Note how, in figure 2.4, the mortar joints appear in a lighter shade of gray (more luminance) than the faces of the brick. Left alone for use as a bump map, the mortar joints appear bumped out when you render, and of course that looks wrong. You can fix this problem two ways. You can "Invert" the image while still in the paint program, which reverses the luminance value for each pixel, and then use this second image as the bump map. Or you can fix it more efficiently in 3D Studio, as described in the following steps.

3. In the Materials Editor module of 3D Studio, load the brick bitmap as both the map file for the brick material's texture and bump maps.

4. Adjust the Amount slider for the bump map down to 25 percent.

5. Click on the Settings button beside the button for the map file you just loaded, then click on the Negative button. When activated, Negative reverses the color values of the bitmap.

Reversing the color values of the bump map image corrects the problem with the mortar joint. To further refine the effect, you can experiment with the Blur slider in the Mapping Parameters dialog box (see fig. 2.5) to soften the edges of the bump map. The idea is to create a smoother transition between the brick and the mortar.

Figure 2.4
The brick texture converted to a 256 grayscale bitmap.

Figure 2.5
The Mapping Parameters dialog box with the Negative button activated and Blur increased to 20.

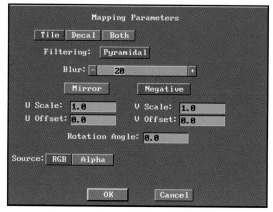

Tip

Increasing the Blur value when creating an animated walkthrough or fly-by for output to video helps eliminate scintillating pixels on the bump map.

You can see in figure 2.6 that the mortar joints properly appear indented from the face of the brick. This effect is fairly simple, but more closely simulates the surface of a real-world brick column, which subtly adds to the realism of the entire scene. You can apply this technique to any type of masonry or tile texture to easily enhance the simulation of split-faced block, textured block, brick, stone, and any type of tile.

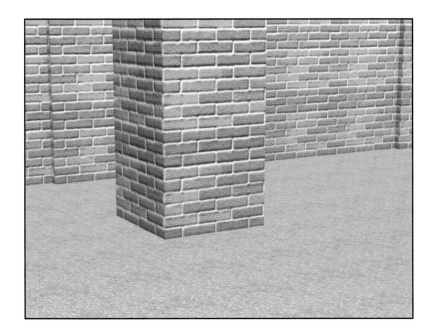

Lofted Mapping

3D Studio enables you to apply mapping coordinates to an object while lofting it. When you choose Objects/Make in the 3D Lofter module, 3D Studio gives you the option to turn on Mapping. Choosing to do so opens the mapping coordinates dialog box (see fig. 2.7).

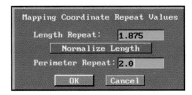

Figure 2.7
3D Lofter's mapping coordinates dialog box.

The Length Repeat and Perimeter Repeat values enable you to set how many times the bitmapped material, assigned to the object later in the 3D Editor, will be repeated along the length and the perimeter of the object. Activating the Normalize Length button tells 3D Studio to scale the bitmap evenly along the length of the lofting path. If you turn off Normalize Length, 3D Studio scales the bitmap unevenly relative to the spacing of the vertices on the lofting path. Except for extreme cases, you do want to turn on the Normalize Length button, especially if working with masonry type textures.

In newer versions of 3D Studio (Release 3 and newer), using the UV Scale and Offset values in the Mapping Parameters dialog box (refer to figure 2.5) accomplishes the same thing, and offers greater flexibility later during the project. You can modify the UV Scale and Offset values anytime during the project, whereas you set the Length Repeat and Perimeter Repeat when you loft the object and cannot change them later.

Masonry Textures—To Scale

One of the first things the viewer will notice about a rendering of a building with brick or masonry components is whether the masonry texture is scaled proportionally with the rest of the model. You can use lofted mapping coordinates to apply perfectly scaled masonry textures to your model.

Although using the UV Scale and Offset values offers greater flexibility for most applications, the UV values are arbitrary and share no correlation with the unit dimensions of the geometry in the 3D Editor.

Using lofted mapping coordinates, therefore, offers just the solution necessary for accurate architectural renderings, as the following illustrates.

Take a column similar to the one shown in figures 2.3 and 2.6 (that is, in the 3D Editor), 3'-4" wide both ways, and 10'-0" tall. Standard CMUs (Concrete Masonry Units), or concrete blocks, are roughly 8" tall and 16" long (measured from the centerlines of the mortar joints).

Figure 2.8
The concrete block bitmap to be mapped to the column.

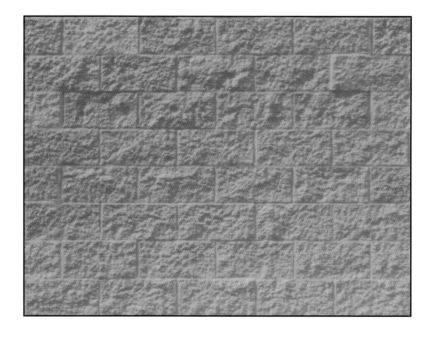

Before you can use the Length Repeat and Perimeter Repeat values in the 3D Lofter, you need to determine how many times to repeat the bitmap for the column, shown in figure 2.9, so that the blocks in the image render to scale at 8" tall and 16" long. To calculate that figure, follow these steps:

1. Divide 8", the height of a block course, into 10'-0", the height of the column. That gives you 15 block courses.

2. Eight courses of block are visible in the bitmap in figure 2.8, so divide the total number of courses you need, 15, by 8. This gives you a result of 1.875; enter that value for the Length Repeat field.

3. Divide 16", the length of a block, into 13'-4", the perimeter of the column. The result is 10, which is the number of block lengths you need for the perimeter.

4. The bitmap is 5 blocks wide, so divide 10 by 5, which yields 2. Enter this value in the Perimeter Repeat field for the number of times 3D Studio needs to repeat the bitmap around the perimeter of the column.

For the concrete block material to be properly mapped to the column, 3D Studio requires twice as many vertices along the perimeter of the shape as the value in the Perimeter Repeat field. In this example, the shape to be lofted is a square, so it already has 4 vertices, twice the needed Perimeter Repeat value of 2, so no extra shape steps are necessary. Unless the path is closed, and this one is open, 3D Studio enforces no restrictions on the number of vertices or steps along the length of the path itself.

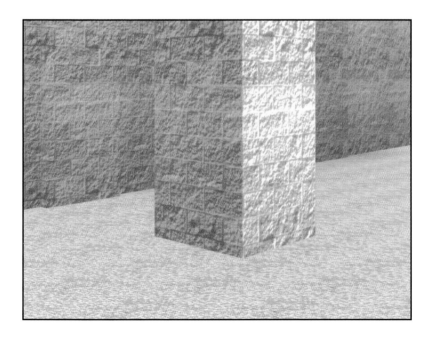

Figure 2.9
Rendering of column with concrete blocks shown to scale, thanks to the use of lofted mapping coordinates.

Using lofted mapping coordinates, you can correctly apply tiling masonry textures to shapes much more complex than the simple square used in the preceding example. An entire facade can be lofted and mapped at once, even if the wall's footprint shape is highly complex. Each turn of the wall's surface will be properly mapped with the chosen texture. This can save you a great deal of time, alleviating the need to physically move and rotate the mapping icon in the 3D Editor for each change in the direction of the wall's surface.

TIP

What if you are importing 3D geometry created in another program, such as AutoCAD, and are therefore unable to use lofted mapping coordinates? Using techniques similar to those used to calculate the necessary bitmap repeat values in the preceding exercise, you can create a reference box object of appropriate dimensions so that the masonry texture would tile exactly once across one of its faces properly scaled. To scale the mapping icon to the face of the box in the 3D Editor, select Surface/Mapping/Adjust/Scale, then click on the box in the appropriate view while holding down the Alt key on the keyboard. The mapping icon is scaled exactly to the size of the box's face. You can then move and rotate the properly scaled mapping icon around as needed in the scene.

Opacity Mapping

Opacity maps control the transparency of the surface of the object to which you apply them. Opacity maps are similar to bump maps in that 3D Studio recognizes only the luminance portion of the bitmap when it calculates opacity. It considers black pixels fully transparent and white pixels fully opaque. The 254 luminance values that fall between black and white represent varying percentages of transparency, much the same way they determine the degree of bumpiness for bump maps.

Fencing in architectural renderings is one area in which using opacity maps can create a very nice effect, as the following example shows.

All you need in the 3D Editor, as far as geometry goes, is a simple set of 2D faces to which you can apply the texture shown in figure 2.10. The bitmap in figure 2.11 serves as the opacity map. As you can see, the areas that need to be transparent for the fence to look real are black. The actual chain link part of the image is white to create the desired opaque effect. The application of this effect is quite simple.

1. In the Materials Editor, assign the fence bitmap shown in figure 2.10 as the map file for Texture 1.

2. Assign the bitmap shown in figure 2.11 as the map file for the opacity map.

3. Set the Amount slider for both to 100 percent.

4. Put the new material in the scene and apply it to the 3D object.

   To increase the visibility of the chain-link fencing, you can combine mapping types, using the same bitmap.

Figure 2.10
The chain-link fence bitmap.

Figure 2.11
The corresponding bitmap for use as the opacity map.

5. Assign the bitmap shown in figure 2.11 as the map file for the bump map.

6. Assign the same bitmap as the map file for the shininess map.

7. Set the Amount slider for both to 100 percent.

8. Put the material to the scene again to replace the previous material.

The finished product should look something like figure 2.12.

Figure 2.12

A closer view of the chain-link fencing in the scene.

You can use opacity maps, along with their corresponding masks, to create powerful effects when you render such things as shrubs and trees, etched glass, signage, decals, graffiti, painted labels, and murals for your architectural presentation.

Shininess Mapping

Shininess maps alter the shininess of materials based upon the variations in luminance, or intensity, of the bitmapped image used as the map. Shininess maps modify the effects of the Material Editor's Shininess and Shininess Strength settings. They do not create or increase the shininess of a material and have no affect on materials that do not already have shininess values applied.

No surface in the real world has a perfectly uniform surface shininess, or gloss. Minute variations occur across every surface due to scratches, weathering, age, and wear. Even the acts of dusting and polishing leave discernable marks. Failure to take this into consideration can make your rendering look too "clean" and computerized. Note how, in the following example, the application of a simple shininess map can change that.

Note how the shine on the conference table in figure 2.13 looks unrealistic. The shine is so strong it almost takes over the scene and is distracting. To tone the shininess down, use a shininess map. Included with 3D Studio are several good bitmaps which can be used to realistically vary the shininess, and one of these, REFMAP.GIF, is used in the following example.

1. In the Materials Editor, assign REFMAP.GIF as the map file for the shininess map for the table material.

2. Set the Amount slider to 75 percent, to help tone down the shine even in places where the map allows for full shininess.

3. Click on the Settings button for the shininess map file, and set both the U and V Scale values to 2.0. Doubling the scale of the map noticeably reduces the bitmap's tiling effect in the rendering.

4. Put the new material in the scene to update the old table's material.

Figure 2.13
A conference table with a perfect shine looking too "clean."

The new version of the rendering, as shown in figure 2.14, looks much more realistic. The shine on the table doesn't seem to dominate the scene anymore, but now adds an additional touch of realism.

Figure 2.14
*The conference table ren-
dered again, this time with
the addition of a shininess
map.*

Final Considerations

There are a few things to always keep in mind when texture mapping that will make the whole process more productive and efficient. The effects your textures and materials will have on the look of the final scene, your RAM usage, and the final rendering time, should be considered during every stage of the project.

Output Type and Resolution

As soon as you can, determine the form the final presentation will take. That enables you to make time-saving decisions early in the project, and not only for materials usage. Ask yourself some questions:

◆ Will the final presentation be an image or an animation?

◆ If it's a single rendered image, what will the output device be, and what is its resolution? How big will the final output be, a standard 8.5"×11" print, or will it be a 24"×36" poster print? How closely will the audience be able to view the final print?

◆ If it's an animation, what is the resolution of the frame buffer? How close will the camera come to different objects and their materials?

You might find that after some planning, some objects might never even show up in the final rendering and therefore don't even need a material. Or some objects that aren't the focus of the scene and are not close to the camera might not even need to have bitmapped materials applied at all. Before texture mapping an object, consider how close the camera will view the object and its associated texture in the final rendering, and compare that to the resolution of the final output. If the final output will be on a computer monitor with a resolution of 1,024×768 pixels, then a brick texture mapped to a distant background object might not even show up recognizably, because the image of each individual brick would be smaller than a single pixel on the computer screen. A simple color material approximating the general color of the bitmap texture might suffice.

Spending a little time up front considering these things can save you a lot of time and unnecessary work during the project, and can speed up the rendering process when you are ready to make the final presentation.

RAM and Rendering Time

As you are using and creating textures, remember that the size and number of bitmaps used in a scene has a definite effect on how much RAM is needed and how long it takes to render. 3D Studio loads all bitmaps referenced in the scene into RAM at render time. If 3D Studio runs out of available RAM, it creates a virtual memory swap file on your hard disk (if you run out of hard disk space, 3D Studio crashes). Paging out to a swap file on your hard disk can dramatically increase the time it takes to render a scene, sometimes taking as much as two to five times longer to render than if you stay within the limits of available RAM. Therefore, care needs to be taken so as not to needlessly fill a scene with too many high-resolution bitmaps.

When 3D Studio loads a bitmap, it automatically converts it to a 24-bit image. So using images with less color depth will not reduce the amount of RAM needed, it will only save hard disk storage space. To find out how much RAM you need for your bitmaps, keep in mind that 24-bit images require about 3 bytes of memory for each pixel. For instance, if you have an image with a resolution of 640×480, to find the necessary RAM multiply the number of pixels by 3 bytes, or (640×480)×3, which means you need about 921 KB of memory. Add up the memory requirements for all the bitmaps you reference in the scene, and you get an idea of how much RAM you need in your system. Also remember that there are other things that take up RAM when you are rendering as well, such as the geometry itself, any object instances in the Keyframer, the output image you are rendering to, the background image, shadows, antialiasing, and so on.

One solution is to make and use more efficient bitmaps. Remember the bitmap used for the ribbed metal panels, shown in figure 2.1? Well, it is not as efficient as it could be. The bitmap in figure 2.15 accomplishes the same thing while using far less hard disk space and RAM. Notice also that the fence bitmaps, figures 2.10 and 2.11, are highly repetitive, and could be modified for further efficiency.

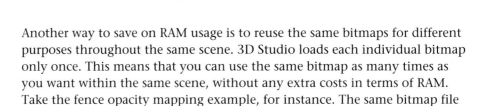

Another way to save on RAM usage is to reuse the same bitmaps for different purposes throughout the same scene. 3D Studio loads each individual bitmap only once. This means that you can use the same bitmap as many times as you want within the same scene, without any extra costs in terms of RAM. Take the fence opacity mapping example, for instance. The same bitmap file was used three times, as the opacity, bump, and shininess maps, but was only loaded into memory once.

Aside from purchasing more RAM for your computer (or buying a faster computer), optimizing your materials for efficiency will go a long way towards keeping your rendering times down, thereby minimizing the amount of time your computer is unusable for things other than rendering.

Summary

The textures and mapping types discussed in this chapter barely scratch the surface of what 3D Studio offers to those seeking to create realistic architectural visualizations. However, this brief look at the use of textures and materials offers a glimpse of what is possible. The only limitation is your own imagination (and, of course, your client's deadline).

Experiment with combining different mapping techniques; this is where the real power lies to enhance the realistic appearance of models and scenes. The many mapping types, along with their associated masks, can be combined in endless ways to produce beautifully detailed renderings.

Take the time to observe the world around you closely. Look at how different lighting situations affect real-world materials and colors. Examine the reflections and surface characteristics of glass and other shiny materials. Take a close look at how dirt and scuff marks affect the shininess or reflectivity of objects around you. The more you learn about and understand how materials in the real world react to, or affect, their environment, the more adept you will become at creating realistic visualizations that convincingly convey your ideas to the audience.

Interiors and Walkthroughs

Chapter 3

by Adam Noble

San Francisco, California

Author Bio

An architecture graduate of the University of California at Berkeley, Adam Noble is Senior Production Manager for CADP, Inc., a San Francisco consulting firm specializing in technical visualization and multimedia animation.

Adam would like to thank Autodesk Inc., V-Consulting, Lightscape Technologies Inc., and the staff at CADP, Inc. for making this chapter possible.

Chapter Overview

This chapter examines methods and techniques for producing professional and communicative architectural visualizations; specifically, interiors and walkthroughs. I use examples from professional work produced by CADP, Inc., to delve into the steps necessary to produce compelling and successful architectural visualization. Specific topics include the following:

◆ Creating effective interior models

◆ Lighting for effect and realism

◆ Animating an interior environment

◆ Postproducing animations

A successful architectural visualization conveys your design solution in an accurate and realistic way to the prescribed audience. To this end, realism, often referred to as *photorealism*, is becoming the aesthetic goal. At CADP, Inc., we strive to add an extra level of realism to our architectural stills and animations. Consequently, this chapter focuses on an animation we produced of a house in Oakland, California, for which the client was interested in visualizing remodeling work. The project, referred to herein as the Kennedy Residence, proved very successful for both the client and CADP, and won the Architectural Visualization category at the 1994 Autodesk Image Awards.

Creating Effective Interior Models

The key to creating an effective interior model is to try to incorporate all the elements the viewer would expect to see in the real world. The visual experience is much more compelling and realistic if you effectively fool the audience into believing this space actually does exist. Two particularly effective techniques for achieving this goal are adding model geometry detail and creating a false exterior environment.

Adding Detail to the Interior Shell

3D Studio's power in 3D model generation often is overlooked and underestimated. You can look at the Kennedy Residence den interior model to see just how geometry detail can enhance the visual experience of a rendered scene. This chapter steps you through a series of images that progressively show architectural elements enhancing the realism of the interior.

Architectural detail is one of the most effective ways and often overlooked techniques for producing compelling interior environments. Too often, modelers fail to include enough elements to produce a realistic environment. Architects and interior designers are particularly acute at recognizing the absence of these architectural details, being trained in the methods of construction and design. But even a lay person can quickly realize something is missing in a scene. Therefore, let's look at the following list of architectural elements included in the Kennedy Residence interior for realism and detail.

- Trim and moldings

- Fixtures

- Furniture

- Plants

- Wall covering

- Fireplace

The principal success to the room's realism, on a modeling level, is attributed to the inclusion of the preceding architectural details and the effectiveness of the materials and textures applied to them. Look closely at figure 3.1 of the den area of the house. All the elements you would expect in the real world seem to be present and accounted for within the model. Trim and moldings are present at floor window and wall intersections. Recessed lights puncture the ceiling, and furniture and plants are placed throughout the space, ultimately enhancing the room's sense of character and depth.

Figure 3.1

The detail of the Kennedy Residence den contributes greatly to the room's realism.

In addition, a fireplace in the corner of the living room brings a sense of hominess and warmth to the space. Not only is the fireplace modeled and a brick texture applied, but a warm crackling fire appears to be burning within it. Later in this chapter, we show you how the fireplace adds a tremendous amount of realism to the animation. First, however, take a look at a few of the techniques used to implement these architectural details.

Trim and Moldings

Topping the list of often overlooked architectural elements are trim and molding. Walls meet floors, ceilings meet walls, doors and windows puncture walls, and more often than not some sort of trim or molding is present at the intersection. Investing a little more time to model these details can add considerable realism to the final visualization. For example, compare the two renderings of the den shown in figures 3.1 and 3.2.

Figure 3.2
The absence of a few simple details greatly reduces the room's realism.

What's missing? Certainly figure 3.1 seems more realistic than figure 3.2. Now, let's examine how including the following architectural elements in the Kennedy Residence enhanced the final realism of the visualization.

Start by looking at how to generate trim and molding quickly using the Shaper and Lofter. One of the principal advantages of lofting geometry is that the mapping coordinates get embedded into the object during creation. Furthermore, generating a path that moves around the perimeter of the space at the wall enables you to generate horizontal molding quickly and easily. One important problem you want to avoid overlooking, however, occurs during lofting. During lofting of a cross section, deformations in sectional width can occur during angular changes. Figure 3.3 shows an example of a simple wall section lofted about this rectangular plan. Notice the varying widths along the wall as it moves about the path. The designer certainly doesn't intend this. So how is this deformation problem corrected?

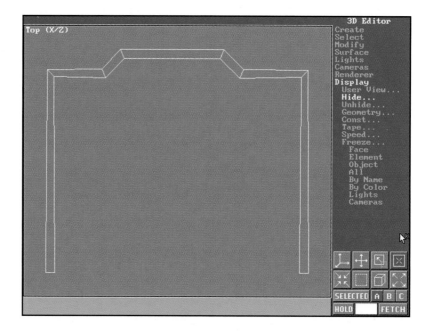

Fortunately, Phillip Miller of Autodesk, Inc., has saved the day and solved this problem. You can use scale factors to correct the width owing to rotation, and thereby generate an accurate perimeter shape. For further exploration into Phillip Miller's solution, see New Riders Publishing's *3D Studio Special Effects*.

Another quick technique that many 3D Studio modelers overlook is vertex manipulation. Creating a quick shape of approximated size and then selecting and moving vertices to size the shape to your model is a fast and effective way to create geometry. Remember, however, when you alter an object with embedded mapping coordinates, the resulting normalization of the map might surprise you. Figure 3.4 shows a lofted rectangle that has been stretched by vertex movement in the Editor. Note the difference between the stretched rectangle and its original shape.

We used Editor's geometry creation and vertex manipulation to create the trim in the den and living room of the Kennedy Residence. One immediate pitfall of this technique is that you have to go back through the model and assign mapping coordinates. You can, however, use a rather straightforward technique to do so. Follow the simple tutorial to discover an easy way to apply consistent mapping coordinates to wall geometry.

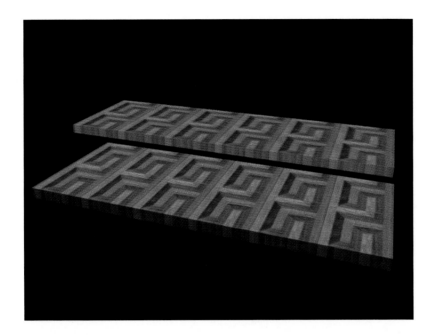

Figure 3.4
*See how the rectangles
look different?*

1. Create a rectangular room consisting of four walls and a bay, as seen in figure 3.5.

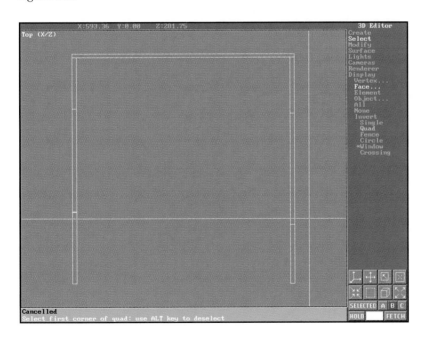

Figure 3.5
*Walls from the Kennedy
Residence den.*

2. From the Top viewport, choose Select/Faces/Window and select all faces parallel to the X axis.

3. Next, choose Modify/Faces/Detach, click on the Selected radio button, and click in the Top viewport.

4. After you detach the faces parallel to the Y axis and create a new object, name it WALL_x.

5. Choose Display/Object/Hide/By Name and hide the object WALL_x.

6. From the Top viewport, choose Select/Face/Window and select all faces parallel to the Y axis (see fig. 3.6).

Figure 3.6

Faces parallel to the Y axis are selected and ready to detach.

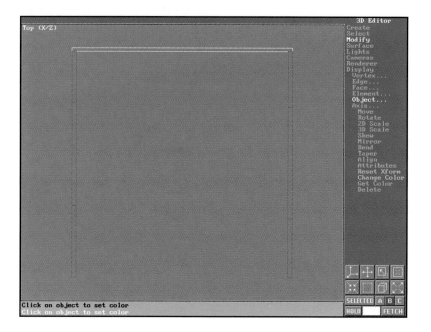

7. Choose Modify/Faces/Detach, click on the Selected radio button, and click in the Top viewport.

8. After you detach the faces parallel to the Y axis and create a new object, name it WALL_y.

9. Choose Display/Object/Hide/By Name and hide the object WALL_x.

You now can see only the walls at 45 degrees and 135 degrees of the X axis. Repeat the preceding steps 6 through 8 to detach each of the these walls, then choose Display/Objects/All.

Now you're ready to assign mapping coordinates to the wall objects.

1. First, activate the Front viewport and look at the object WALL_x. Lights have already been set up and the default material still is applied to all the wall objects. Choose Surface/Materials/Get Library and select WALLS.MLI.

2. Choose Surface/Material/Get and select a suitable wall material with a referenced map.

3. Next, apply the material to all wall objects. Choose Surface/Material/ Assign/Object/By Name and select the ALL radio button in the object selection dialog box.

4. View the bitmap used as a texture map in the material you have selected, and choose Render/View/Bitmap. You map this texture along the walls to create, in our case, a paneled wall look.

5. Choose Surface/Mapping/Find Icon, press Ctrl+Z to zoom extent, and click in the Front viewport. The mapping coordinate icon appears in the Front viewport.

Next, you size the coordinate to a suitable shape for tiling the wood panel effect.

6. Under Surface/Mapping/Bitmap Fit, resize the icon to get it into the same aspect ratio as the texture referenced by your material. In other words, this will force the width-to-height ratio of the mapping icon to be that of your bitmap.

7. Align the mapping icon to a face of the WALL_x object so you can keep track of the icon's location. Choose Surface/Mapping/Align To Face and select a face on object WALL_x. Make sure the face is parallel to the X axis.

8. From the Front viewport, scale in all directions the icon to WALL_x's full height, choose Surface/Mapping/Apply/Object, and select WALL_x in the object selection dialog box.

Render the Front viewport and see if you like the paneling's scale. If not, rescale the icon and reapply the coordinate to the object until you do like it. After you're satisfied with the result, the next steps involve rotating the icon and applying it to the other walls.

1. From the Top viewport, choose Surface/Mapping/Rotate, click in the Top viewport, and rotate the mapping icon 90 degrees clockwise. Use the numbers in the menu bar to verify a 90-degree rotation.

2. Apply the mapping coordinates to the WALL_y object.

3. Press C and view the wall's object from a camera already set up in the scene and render.

All the walls now have consistent mapping coordinates applied to them. This same technique works well setting up mapping coordinates for pitched floors with shingle textures. Remember the Surface/Mapping/Face Align command when applying mapping coordinates to sloped objects.

Fixtures, Furnishings, and Plants

Another effective way to bring life to an environment is to use fixtures and furnishings. Fixtures and furnishings add scale and depth to an interior space. Scale is particularly important, because viewers cannot easily respond cognitively to the size and feel of an animation's virtual environment without points of reference. Furniture and fixtures help generate the illusion of depth and additional realism to the interior by providing points of reference and objects of focus. Therefore, experiment with adding these design details to your interiors.

The more details you add to your interior, the more realistic your animation. Look at the room you're in now and notice all the elements that surround you—moldings, trim, light fixtures, outlets, and wall coverings, among others.

Autodesk, as well as other third-party companies, produces furniture and miscellaneous geometry (available on CD-ROM) that you can use to spice up an environment. Autodesk's *3D Props Residential and 3D Props Commercial* is an excellent source for such models. Utilizing third-party geometry can help you produce faster and create more compelling visualizations. Be forewarned, however, that you often need to use materials and textures to adjust and customize the models to achieve the results you want. Any animator eventually begins to generate personally customized model libraries of fixtures, furnishing, and whathaveyou for use in future projects. Save your models; they might come in handy down the road. The Kennedy Residence consists primarily of models generated entirely in-house.

The hutch and bookcase, for example, were designed and modeled specifically for the den. Examining how we did it reveals how mapping and texture detail can enhance the visualization. In this case, we combined the wood texture map with mapping that miters each joint to bring out extra realism. Figures 3.7 and 3.8 illustrate how the detailed texture mapping of the wood grain adds realism to the rendering.

Textures and Mapping

Texture mapping and material definition is a critical step for producing compelling visualization. 3D Studio offers several controls you can use to define a material's properties. The three color sliders, Ambient, Diffuse, and Specular, enable you to control the material's color in particular lighting conditions, whereas the Shininess and Transparency sliders allow for more advanced definitions. None of these controls, however, enable you to produce more realistic imagery than you can simply by using texture mapping. Texture mapping enables the architect, or designer, to bridge the gap between traditional renderings and communicate a more realistic vision of the design. This is the "photo" process of creating photorealistic visualization.

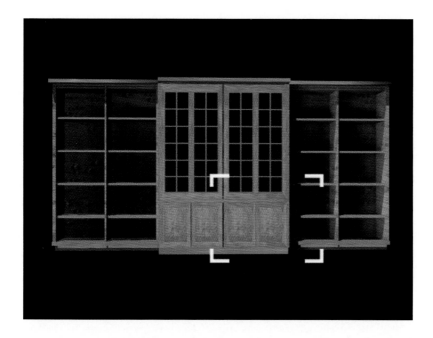

Figure 3.7
The final mapping and material settings of the hutch.

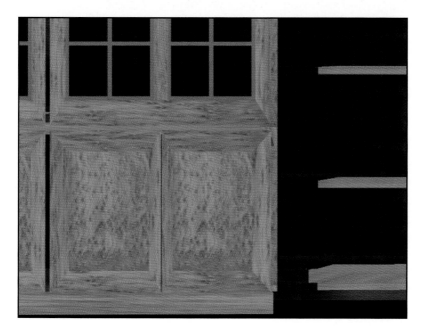

Figure 3.8
Wood grain miter joint texture mapping in detail contributes to the realism of the hutch.

Most architectural firms have material libraries available for office designers to visually compare and contrast the textures and colors for specification within the design, and then make material specifications based on this visual review. 3D Studio offers this same sort of library in virtual space, and provides even more control. Not only can you select materials, but you can manipulate and apply them to model geometry, as well as view them within the design under different lighting conditions.

Creating a False Exterior

An excellent technique for adding realism to your animation involves using an environment map. You simply find or take a photograph of the view you want outside your interior and map it to a very large cylinder or half sphere. Panoramic cameras are particularly good for this type of use, owing to their large fields of view.

Next, follow along to see how the living room false environment was set up and composited into the final animation. Notice the large dome-like shape that surrounds the house geometry. This dome acts as the holder for the false environment map. We have already imported the camera path from the interior walkthrough and set it up to render. First, however, you need to map the background texture map to the dome.

1. Choose Render/View Image and see figure 3.9. At the prompt, select RESCALE to view the entire map. When composited to the interior scene, the sunset map acts as the false exterior condition in the ultimate animation. Press Esc to return to the Editor.

Figure 3.9

The nighttime bitmap image used for the living room false background environment.

2. Choose Surface/Mapping/Type/Cylindrical, press Ctrl, and click on the dome to size and center a spherical mapping coordinate to the dome.

3. Press F5 to activate the Materials Editor and set up the background material.

4. In the Materials Editor, choose MATERIAL/LIBRARY NEW to create a new materials library.

5. Next choose Texture 1 and load your background image at 100%.

6. Press P to put the material to your new materials library and name the material.

7. Press F3 to return to the Editor and assign the material to the dome object.

8. Press F4 to enter the Keyframer. Set your current frame number to a position in your motion where you can view outside.

In the Keyframer, unhide some of your geometry to use as a visibility reference. This will make finalizing the position of the false background in relation to the interior space considerably easier.

9. Render the Camera viewport. If the background isn't where you want it, rotate the map coordinate in the editor until you like where you have it.

Experiment some; adjust the scale and rotatation of the mapping coordinate until the map appears in the location you want. Make sure that no seams are visible from within your interior camera path. Mirroring the map can reduce the visual impact of seams if you simply cannot avoid edges. Try to view the background from several frames throughout the animation to avoid edges or surprising results.

This mapped-dome technique works especially well in movement because the distant map seen through windows or openings enhances the scene's depth. Furthermore, try using the Mapping Parameters dialog box to blur the environment map, which also enhances the viewer's perception of depth and realism.

Compositing Interiors and Exteriors

The next set of steps shows you how to use Video Post to composit the background rendering and the interior rendering.

1. Enter into the Keyframer of 3D Studio.

2. Choose Info/Configure/Map Paths from the menu bar and find the appropriate directory where 3D Studio can find the referenced map. Then choose OK three times to return to the Keyframer.

3. Choose Render/Video Post, select ADD, and click twice to add two [KF SCENE] entries.

4. Choose EDIT and select the top [KF SCENE] entry. After the Queue Entry dialog box opens, choose BITMAP and select the empty field to the right to load your background image (see fig. 3.10) from the appropriate directory. After you load your background image, choose OK until 3D Studio returns you to Video Post.

Figure 3.10

An example of the Kennedy Residence living room background image uncomposited with the interior.

Next, you load the interior rendering (see fig. 3.11) for composite.

Figure 3.11

The living room interior rendering without the background.

5. Select the second [KF SCENE] entry and choose BITMAP, then load your interior rendering. Click on OK until you return Video Post.

Now, you need to invoke the alpha channel for a clean composite.

6. Select the ALPHA field for your interior render (see fig. 3.12), to open the Alpha dialog box. Choose Queue Alpha, and then choose OK to return once more to Video Post.

Figure 3.12

An example of the 8-bit greyscale alpha channel stripped from the interior rendering.

7. In Video Post, enter **1** in the Frames field and choose SET. Answer YES to the two questions it asks you.

Now you're ready to render the composite.

8. Choose Render and set up the rendering parameters. The images already have been rendered and all you want Video Post to do is composite the two files; therefore, you can set all render settings to OFF.

9. Choose Configure and set to your display driver and enter a resolution of 640×480. Choose OK and return to the Render Video Post Animation dialog box. Now just select Single in the Frames field and RENDER using Video Post.

Video Post should give you a nice composited rendering of the exterior and interior images (see fig. 3.13).

Figure 3.13
*The final composited image
of the Kennedy Residence
living room.*

Most animators use Video Post composites during production of architectural animations to split the interior rendering files from the exterior environment renderings. Compositing allows for better control of the ultimate appearance of the final animation. You can render the time-consuming interior files using alpha, then later composite using an exterior background. Make sure however, that you use the same camera path and coordinate space for both render sets. By using this technique, the animator later can change or fine-tune the background quickly and easily.

For animations, you should make IFL files and composite a series of several files during a single session, rather than load a single file in Video Post. *IFL files* are simple text files that contain a list of bitmap file names that Video Post reads in succesion from the top down. So for example, in the exercise above, you would list the den background files in succession within an IFL file and load them as the first [KF SCENE], while the second field would be the IFL listing of the interior den files with alpha queued.

Lighting for Effect

Lighting an interior scene probably is one of the most intimidating tasks for producers of architectural visualizations. With a good understanding of 3D Studio lighting tools, however the animator can produce realistic interior lighting effects. Remember, because 3D Studio lights don't actually simulate real world lighting and radiosity, the technique is to use whatever tools you have to trick the viewer into believing the lighting is realistic. As in nearly all aspects of 3D Studio visualization production, you spend a considerable amount of time just testing and tweaking to create good effects. This section focuses on the following topics specific to lighting interiors and will give further insight into some of these tricks you can try to enhance your scenes' lighting.

◆ Ambient light setting

◆ Omni lights

◆ Spotlights

◆ 3D Studio stage lighting for realism

◆ Radiosity and Lightscape rendering solution

At the close of this section, we explore radiosity and the Lightscape rendering package available to animators. Lightscape is a very powerful rendering package that supports 3D Studio models and allows the animator to simulate real world lighting conditions based on illumination datasets.

Looking closer at lighting a scene, we will delve deeper into the Kennedy Residence animation settings. In addition, we will go over how we set up the lights in the Voodoo Lounge project produced at CADP, Inc., in 1994. The Voodoo Lounge client was very interested in "mood" lighting, such as you find in old New Orleans clubs and bars. We employed multiple spot lights in our solution and the project should serve as an excellent example in the study of stage type lighting.

Ambient Light

3D Studio allows for three different light types in a scene: Ambient, Omni, and Spot. Through thorough testing at our office, we have concluded that you achieve the most compelling lighting by enhancing contrast between light and no light. The best technique available for producing this type effect is to keep the ambient light level at 10 or less and liberally use spotlights throughout the scene. Keeping ambient light down and omni lights minimized helps prevent undesirable washing out of the scene. The ambient light setting in the scene is the nondirectional lighting of all objects within the scene. In this case, the ambient is set to 10. Figure 3.14 shows the lighting setup in the Kennedy Residence den.

The ambient level is set very low, so you have to use spots and omni lights to illuminate the geometry. Next, you look closer at lighting in 3D Studio to discover why spotlights are used primarily to light an interior scene. Compare figure 3.15, which shows the final render of the Kennedy Residence den, to figure 3.14, which shows the lighting setup.

Figure 3.14
The lighting setup in the Kennedy Residence den.

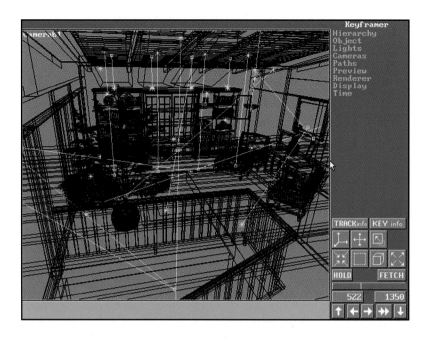

Figure 3.15
The final render of the Kennedy Residence den.

Omni Light

The 3D Studio reference manual describes *omni lights* as "point sources that radiate light rays in all directions equally from a single source." The reference manual goes on to suggest that "most scenes require no more than three omni lights." In actual experience, we rarely use more than two global omni lights and often all others are highly controlled using range and exclusion settings.

Omni lights illuminate any face pointed toward the light source. They don't stop for geometry or distance; therefore, you should use them sparsely and control them tightly. Multiple uncontrolled omni lights can wash out a scene and reduce contrast, creating an effect similar to using a high ambient setting.

Spotlights

As figure 3.14 illustrates, spotlights proved in the Kennedy Residence interior to be the best tool to simulate the desired lighting conditions. A good rule of thumb for setting up spots in an interior environment is to place a spotlight in each light fixture to be turned on for the final rendering, then add stage and effect lighting to achieve the final desired effect. For the Kennedy Residence, we manipulated a single recessed light until the we achieved the settings we wanted, then we cloned the light and moved it to the other recessed light locations. After we made some adjustments to the target of each spotlight, we attained a consistent lighting effect for the recessed lighting condition.

Secondly, by testing and tweaking, we found that the falloff settings for the spotlight should have a value near the hotspot. Tightening the hotspot to falloff distribution enhances the contrast between areas of spotlight and ambient light.

Multipliers add further useful control over the results of spotlights. Often the light is not bright enough or you want a subtle wash of light on a wall or surface. Multipliers provide this control, so experiment with settings between .2 and 10 to get a feel for the range of results. Usually, a spotlight you use to simulate sunlight, for example, has a very high multiplier setting. The sun spotlight in the Kennedy Residence animation has a multiplier value of 5 and is positioned very far away from the model to tighten the hotspot cone to nearly its tightest setting. Setting up the spotlight in this manner simulates a beam of light, such as those the sun produces, directly into your scene. When rendered, you can generate hard-edged shadows, such as those produced by the skylight visible.

At this point, the scene is beginning to look better, but still lacks an overall sense of realism. We needed to add some simple lighting tricks or stage lighting techniques to move this environment to the next level. Just as stage designers use extra lights to add depth and contrast to their environments, so too can the animator of virtual interiors. Notice that several lights in the Voodoo Lounge model (shown in figure 3.16) are positioned on the floor and aimed at the ceiling. The purpose of these spots is to simulate light bouncing off the floor back into the room. Notice also the hotspot to falloff distribution of these lights is set very high to get more of a washing of light rather than a beam effect. A subtle color value in these lights also can add realism to the scene. In effect, the up-spotlight simulates the radiosity properties of light bouncing around a room. Later, we look deeper into radiosity rendering during discussion of the tools available in the Lightscape renderer.

Figure 3.16

*Notice the lighting tech-
niques in the Voodoo
Lounge model.*

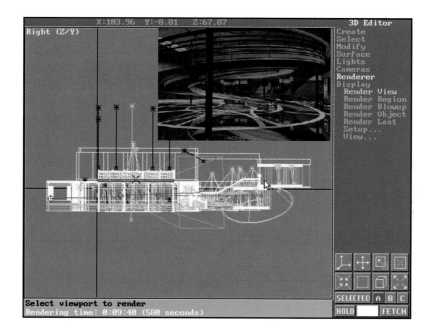

Effect Lighting

The final lighting technique used in the Kennedy Residence visualization is
referred to here as *effects lighting*. In the Kennedy Residence, the fireplace
played a pivotal role as the initial focus of the living room animation. We
wanted to overstate the room's comfort and lived-in feel, so we gave critical
attention to making the fire seem very realistic.

The success of making this particular fire effect ultimately can be attributed
to two effects spotlights. The first is a flickering shadow casting spotlight illu-
minating from the fireplace that bobs up, down, left and right, splashing
irregular shadows about the fireplace area. The second is a projector spotlight
created from the rotoscoped fire flic that gives the impression that light flick-
ers about and licks the adjacent floor and glass. A closer look at the overall
effect of the fireplace removes the mystery from the way it was achieved.

First, we rotoscoped the looping fire from video footage of an actual fireplace.
We mapped this flic file to a planar surface that we placed at the center of the
fireplace and assigned a material with the FIRE.FLC as texture 1 (see fig. 3.17).
Next, we generated a transparency map by converting the fire.flc into an 8-bit
grey scale flic in Animator Pro and simply hand-painting the background
from the original video footage. Combined as an animated texture and opacity map in the materials editor, the fire effect was produced (see fig. 3.18).

Again, the effect just didn't seem to be convincing enough, so we explored
effects lighting in an attempt to simulate the bouncing of light expelled from
a crackling fire.

Figure 3.17
FIRE.FLC as the texture for the fire.

Figure 3.18
FIRE.FLC and opacity mapping in the final fireplace.

The final touches to make the Kennedy Residence complete regarding lighting were applied by employing shadow maps for interior lights and a single ray-traced light that created the illusion of sunlight blasting through the den's sky lights. Understanding the difference between shadow maps and ray traced shadows and the advantages and disadvantages of each cannot be emphasized enough.

Shadow Maps

At CADP, we find that for the complex, messy shadows frequently desired in architectural spaces, the venerable shadow map light can prove quite useful. Unfortunately, even some very sophisticated animators still don't fully comprehend how shadow maps work. This section tries to uncover what shadow maps settings do and how to employ them most efficiently.

The shadow map itself is a bitmap created and held in memory by 3D Studio. When you see the Rendering Shadow Map status bar during a shadows on rendering, 3D Studio is filling in the data for one shadow map in your scene, based on the object's faces that are visible to the spotlight in that frame, given the lights direction and *FOV*. For both image maps and shadow maps, each pixel in the array corresponds to a direction vector. This vector originates at the camera point or spotlight point and travels through a flat projection plane to correspond to the first visible point in the scene. The difference between a typical image bitmap and a shadow map is that the pixels in an image correspond to what color the scene point should be, whereas in the shadow map, each pixel holds a number that represents the distance from the spotlight to the point in the scene.

Most problems with shadow maps arise from the edges of the shadows. Shadows seem to pull away from the object that casts them, have strange banding effects, or be too blurry. They crop up when surfaces that cast shadows come very close to surfaces that receive shadows, or where you have edges in the shadow map.

Shadow maps are impractical in architectural renderings unless you can control the marginal conditions separately. You have two values available for doing this in the Shadow Map Control dialog box: the Bias and the Map Sample Range. The Bias setting is the distance by which the distance recorded in the shadow map pixel must excede the distance measure in the scene. You can think of raising the Bias value as decreasing every distance value in the shadow map by that amount. The distance from scene point to spotlight must exceed the shadow map distance by at least the value of the Bias (see fig. 3.19).

On the other hand, increasing the Sample Range tells 3D Studio to derive the shadow map distance by taking a weighted average of increasingly large sample of pixels about the primary pixel. This avails an efficient way to remove the jagged edges from the map values, resulting in soft, even shadows desirable for interior lighting conditions.

Figure 3.19

An example of a shadow mapping setup dialog box.

For the Kennedy Residence interior, we were sure to adjust the Bias values to avoid the pulling-away effect of shadows from their casting objects. And based on our understanding of shadow maps and their control, we concluded that using a large number of shadow map spotlights with low map sizes but high sample ranges is the most efficient way to populate an interior scene with complex fuzzy shadows.

Ray Trace Shadows

As seen in the Kennedy Residence den, ray traced lights can be very effective for simulating sunlight because they give such clean and sharp shadows, not unlike those you see on a bright, clear day. Ray traced shadows, however, can tax system resources during render time, forcing particular attention to and control of their setup. Further exploration into our particular spotlight settings would reveal that the Exclude button is utilized to reduce the amount of geometry calculated during the generation of the ray traced shadow. Also by reducing the light cone and excluding all geometry the light does not need to affect both limits the calculations performed by the software. The result of such controls can be highly significant speed enhancements during render time.

Remember, also, if you exclude several objects from the ray traced shadow spot, you can always clone the spot and exclude the opposite object in the scene and turn off the shadow casting radio button. This way, the light gets evenly distributed to all objects, but 3D Studio calculates only a subset of the scene's objects during ray tracing, which conserves memory resources and render time.

Radiosity and Lightscape Rendering

Lightscape is a rendering package just made available to 3D Studio and AutoCAD users (see fig. 3.20). Lightscape uses a technology called *radiosity*, originally developed by thermal engineers, to calculate and simulate global illumination effects throughout a defined environment. The radiosity algorithm calculates the propagation of diffuse light within a scene and applies the data directly to the environment's geometry.

The realism of the light distribution in a Lightscape rendered interior is very accurate and convincing. Color bleeding and indirect illumination of surfaces provide a level of realism unachievable using just the 3D Studio rendering engine. Furthermore, Lightscape relies on photometric data sets to calculate illumination levels, expanding its capabilities as a true lighting conditions simulator. You can input illumination data direct from the lighting manufacturer, and control and manipulate it within the software.

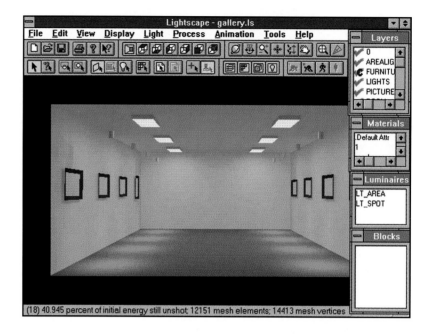

Figure 3.20

The Lightscape Visualization System, showing the interface and an image.

The Lightscape solution is an excellent tool for architects and lighting consultants who need to be particularly sensitive to a scene's interior lighting.

Animating an Interior Environment

Effectively producing communicative architectural visualization is maturized by using animation. With the interior model complete and all materials and lights satisfactorily set, we now are ready to animate a virtual camera throughout the space. This section focuses on the steps used during the Kennedy Residence walkthrough and touches on the following issues.

◆ Communication objectives

◆ Storyboards

◆ Creating motion

◆ Dynamic interiors

◆ Rendering and compositing

Communication Objectives

Before setting up camera paths and animating frames, you should first sketch out the goals you hope to communicate in the final animation. Do you want the piece to be educational or sales-oriented, for example, entertaining or forensic, in nature? Getting a sense of what you want your animation to communicate lends focus to your work. This stage of production can easily get time-consuming and blow schedules and budgets. Remember, animating is when computer resources and render time take on critical importance and must be kept organized and controlled.

After completing the model for the Kennedy Residence, the staff sat down to discuss how to animate the final model. The first question posed was "What is the ultimate goal in producing this animation?" In this case, the answer was two-fold. First, we wanted to demonstrate the effectiveness of realistic computer-generated architectural visualization to clients, and second, we wanted to generate a showpiece for our demo reel that illustrated our company's technical and artistic abilities. Therefore, we stressed realistic generation of lighting and materials, as seen in earlier sections. We felt we needed to animate the space to bring it to life to show off the skillful work we had done during the setup stages. Having determined our objectives, we next began to brainstorm possible movements throughout the space, using storyboards.

Storyboards

Using storyboards is the most effective way to outline an animation. Storyboards are an illustrative technique developed by early cell animators to define particular keyframes in an animation. These keyframes visually describe the key parts of the animation and help define the order and timing of events. Storyboards can be anything from simple sketches laid out on a single piece of paper (see fig. 3.21) to a series of several highly rendered and detailed drawings pinned to a wall. The particular detail of the storyboards is of less importance than the effectiveness of it to outline and define the animated sequence. After discussing and finally agreeing on the storyboards, the animation is set and animators can focus directly on producing the sequences.

A technique used in the Kennedy Residence walkthrough took storyboards a step further in defining details of the animation in the form of what we call a *keyframe outline*. A keyframe outline is a tool our animators used to define the exact timing of events based on the storyboards. Its format simply is a timeline resembling the Track Info dialog box in 3D Studio's Keyframer module. Animators use this timeline to define key frames of events and their durations. In the den sequence of the animation, for example, a sliding glass door shuts during a lighting change from day to night. Using the keyframe outline, animators defined the timing and durations of this movement and began testing and then tweaking the frame numbers based on preview flics until they were satisfied. Therefore, unlike storyboarding, you can change and edit the keyframe outline throughout production as required. Changes then can be communicated easily to other animators working on adjoining sequences.

Figure 3.21

An example of a simple storyboard created for a multimedia animation of a ferryboat and lighthouse.

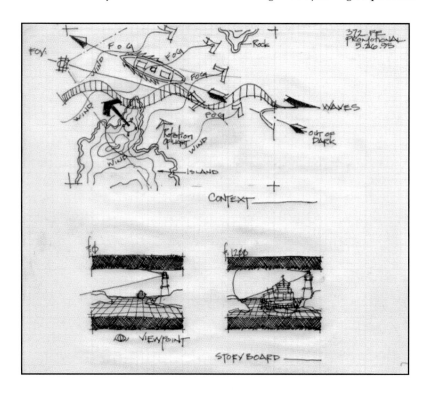

Creating Motion

Creating camera paths can be tricky in an interior environment. A typical approach animators at CADP use is to generate a loose camera that hits the areas that the storyboard has defined in the correct number of frames. Then the animator tests and tweaks to clean up and tighten keyframes within the motion path of the camera and target until satisfying the objectives of the storyboard and achieving smooth, consistent motion.

TIP

Be sure to eliminate all abrupt or jerky camera motion. Jerky camera motion, more than anything else during this stage of production, detracts the viewer's attention from the focus of the animation.

I would suggest liberal use of Preview Flics to test possible motion paths (see fig. 3.22). Also, use the Camera Clone tool and generate several deviations of similar paths, which lets you easily explore changes without losing previous settings. (Holding down the Shift key when moving a camera or target will clone that particular camera.) Furthermore, you should explore different tension, continuity, and bias settings at keyframes along the camera path. If your camera paths are consistently jerky, pay particular attention to the tension settings at the nearest keyframe.

Figure 3.22

A sample image from a motion preview of the den animation.

If at keyframe 100 and keyframe 150 the camera and target positions are locked, for example, under default 3D Studio settings. The camera jerks strangely unless you set the tension spinner to 0. Set up a camera path and experiment with different tension settings at keyframes. Use preview flics to study your results.

The final tool in creating professional-looking camera motion is liberally using Ease To and Ease From spinners. Rarely should your camera come to an abrupt halt or start during motion. Movements such as these surprise and distract the viewer's focus on the interior. Always ease to stops and ease from pauses to keep the viewer's focus on the rendered environment. Smooth and dynamic camera paths can enhance the animation but should do so in a subordinate role to the interior space itself.

Dynamic Interiors

Finally, in generating the animation for the Kennedy Residence, we wanted excitement and realism to be the principal focus of the piece. Because we focused on realism during creation of the model and the material and lighting applied to its surfaces, we wanted to add excitement and movement to the space during the animation stage. We achieved this by including a lighting change from day to night and the movement of the sliding glass door from open to closed (see fig. 3.23).

Figure 3.23

Den frames showing lighting changes and door movement.

By making the interior dynamic, our goal was to keep the viewer alert and intrigued, not only by the interior design, but also by the activity within the space. Some viewers of our animation did comment on the added excitement the door and lighting changes bring to the overall animation. Some even commented on the realism of the composited background sky's orbital movement and color changes.

All of the subtle techniques discussed here might not elevate your animation on their own, but when employed all together can be highly effective. Refer to figure 3.23 to see the lighting changes of the den. Furthermore, notice the clouds in the composited sky change color. Figure 3.24 demonstrates the progressive color change in the sky simulating a sunset effect. The large image shows the daytime sky, with the inset representing the color shifts in the background until it reaches a nighttime feel.

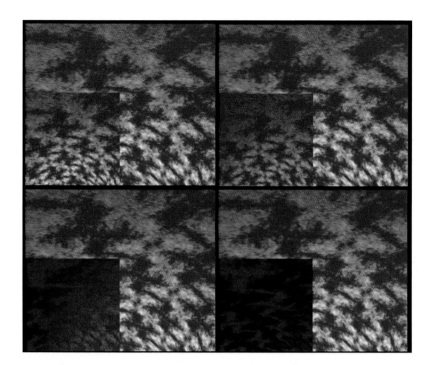

Rendering and Compositing

Now that the camera paths have been set up, it's time to plan and forecast the rendering of the animation. At this stage, the animator turns into a planner and shepherd to the computer settings and speed.

The first step in the Kennedy Residence animation was to verify that the exterior environment's camera and the interior environment's camera were congruent and would allow for seamless compositing during post production. The exterior model was tested for lighting, and stills were composited until we liked the final look and feel of the images. We then merged the final camera into the model and set up the exterior to be rendered. Next, we had to make decisions regarding how to render the ultimate animation. Specifically, we had to weigh and answer the following five matters before preceding:

- ◆ Forecasting render time

- ◆ Frame or field rendering

- ◆ Alpha

- ◆ Output resolution and file format

- ◆ Gamma setting

Allowable Render Times

Forecasting and planning the system resources and time constraints associated with rendering an animation is critical to its success. You can easily blow budgets and deadlines by not including how long the animation will take to render in your advance forecasting.

To generate forecasts, render every 25th, 50th, or 100th frame and quarry the times associated with each, then derive an estimated average render time per frame. Multiply that average figure by the number of frames in your scene to get an estimated number of machine hours to render the entire animation. If you then divide that number by the number of machines dedicated to rendering the scene, you get an estimate for how many hours or days the rendering will take. Remember, however, that if you have a network of different computer configurations, you must perform frame time testing for each machine if you want or need to increase the accuracy of your forecast.

Furthermore, in the Kennedy Residence case, we wanted the extra smoothness of motion achieved through field rendering, so we tested render times for both frames and fields. Fields render a percentage slower than frames, and you should always consider them as well when you do your time forecasts.

Frame and Field Rendering

Field rendering can add smoothness to animated motion, at the expense of additional render time. When rendering fields, the render generates two fields per frame of alternating scan lines. These fields then increase the frame rate, for example, from NTSC 30 Frames/sec to 60 Fields/sec. The resulting movement of the animated motion appears smoother. You should use field rendering if your system resources can allow for the additional render time, but you should consider several things in deciding whether to render fields.

Having fields set to On works only for frame rendering and should never be set when rendering a flic. Second, be aware of the field order in the 3D Studio 3DS.SET file. The setting is either 0 or 1 and controls which scan line of the field renders first. You can perform simple animation tests to verify field order setting to avoid any mistakes. The frames will strobe if the field order is reversed. If for any reason, you render a series of frames in descending order, you must also reverse the field order.

Alpha

Next, before rendering your animation, you will have to decide whether you need alpha information in addition to your image files. Alpha is an 8-bit file that represents—through levels of gray—how much transparency each pixel should carry (where black is 100% transparent and white is 100% opaque). This alpha information then allows you to utilize a transparency channel in postproduction. In the Kennedy Residence, for example, interior frames were rendered with an alpha on and later composited with a congruent set of background renderings. Then during rendering, each 24-bit frame had an 8-bit alpha or transparency channel embedded. Having alpha information available within each frame allowed our animators to cleanly composite the false background and sky in video post with the interior renders. Alpha information can also be set to alpha split. This generates a series of 8-bit alpha files unembedded with your frames. The advantage of alpha split is that it enables you to freely manipulate the alpha channel series if you need to before reassociating them with their associated 24-bit frames.

Output Resolution and File Format

Deciding on the resolution and format to render an animation depends on how the client ultimately will view the animation. Again, in the case of our walkthrough, our objective was to include the sequence on a company demo reel. For viewing ease and distribution costs, we decided the demo reel would be VHS. Furthermore, because in-house we master animation frame-by-frame on a BetaCAM SP VTR with a TARGA PLUS frame buffer, the resolution question was answered by the hardware and output selection. All fields were rendered at 512×486, which is the maximum limit of the TARGA PLUS and NTSC. Furthermore, we rendered each field in TARGA format with alpha on, which allowed us to composite the background files in Video Post.

Rendering 32-bit TARGA interior files and 24-bit TARGA exterior files taxed our resources considerably. We had to allocate and reserve hundreds of megabytes of disk space and backup tape for the entire animation. Animators should often consider using JPEG files if available resources are limited. The advantage of JPEG in file size and required disk space can be dramatic. Even when JPEG quality settings are set to 99%, the compression on each file is significant over TARGA or TIFF. Remember, however, that JPEG files don't allow let you use alpha information, so if you will need to composite frames, you must use TARGA or TIFF.

Gamma

The final issue in rendering the final animation is to properly set the Gamma control. Gamma is a function that is applied to the RGB values in a bitmap to correct its range of intensities so that it appears correctly when output on a particular device (such as a screen, printer, frame buffer, or video monitor). Gamma frequently is graphically represented as a bow-shaped curve indicating what gamma changes are made at intermediate values between absolute dark and absolute bright. This gamma curve is best depicted by the adjustments available within PhotoStyler, an image editing program (see fig. 3.25).

Figure 3.25

*The gamma adjustments
available within Adobe's
PhotoStyler image editing
program.*

Note the following three aspects of Gamma:

♦ Gamma correction is necessary, but the final setting is ultimately a subjective decision.

♦ Different gamma settings are appropriate to the same bitmap, depending on the hardware used to view it.

♦ Gamma correction can be made before rendering (lighting and material settings) and/or after rendering (by imposing a gamma setting on the rendered frame).

We have found that the best strategy for gamma is to experiment with the various output devices you intend to use and nail down your gamma settings on all machines. Remember, gamma is a setting that helps you control the intermediate brightness values of your images for a particular output device. Utilize it to your advantage to avoid washed out or overly dark images.

Directing and Editing

Finally, you have generated a model, assigned materials, set up lights and cameras, and rendered all your frames. Now you're ready to put together all your work into a professional presentation.

A typical presentation starts with titling and transitional fade describing the project. Always use a fade between titling for a more professional look. Furthermore, remember your safe frame limits when generating titles. You want to avoid at all costs titles appearing too close or over the border of your display limits. Experiment with exiting title at different sizes and locations. Remember, you are the director.

Animators often overlook the use of cut edits in animated walkthroughs. A *cut edit* is an unfaded cut from one scene to the next. Cut edits between moving scenes seem to work better than from moving to still. Set up and test possible edits in Video Post at low resolution to determine whether you should fade a transition or simply cut from one to the next. Transitional effects can bring excitement to the final presentation but should be scoped out during the storyboard process to avoid rendering additional frames for postproduction.

Output

Deciding on a suitable format to output the final animation should be, as mentioned earlier, decided on before rendering. A variety of formats can serve to display animation. Choosing the best for your particular purposes can assure that your client can view the final product easily and that you can distribute the animation to market your work.

Our office primarily produces animation for BetaCAM SP mastering at 30 frames/second or 60 fields/second NTSC. We use this output format because it allows for easy VHS dubbing from the BetaSP master, which makes for low cost and effective distribution. Also, by having the Beta master, the animation is always suitable for broadcast.

Summary

You can employ a variety of methods and techniques during the production process to generate more compelling architectural visualizations and walk-throughs. Thoroughness and attention to detail can enhance your models and material texturing. Carefully organizing storyboards and rendering can increase focus and help stay within budget. And finally, a suitable output device to display and distribute the final visualization will satisfy the client and advance your marketability.

Producing first-rate professional architectural visualizations requires organization, planning, testing, and patience, so don't get discouraged if at first you do not succeed. Continue to test and experiment, and eventually you will be fluid enough with the software to effectively render and animate architectural spaces.

Exteriors and Fly-Bys

by Jesse K. Miguel, AIA
Boston, Massachusetts

Author Bio

Jesse K. Miguel, AIA, is a Project Designer/Architectural CAD Coordinator for the architectural/engineering firm of HNTB in Boston, Massachusetts. He is in charge of 3D design on the computer, using Autodesk's AutoCAD and 3D Studio to create 3D computer models for photorealistic still images and computer animation. He is also responsible for overseeing the AutoCAD operations, setting project standards, creating CAD files, and serving as the Architectural Group's CAD client contact. Mr. Miguel has recently been named the 3D Rendering and Animation Manager for HNTB at their Kansas City, Missouri, headquarters, where he will be directing the development of 3D computer graphics and animation in the Technical Computer Support Group of HNTB, as well as providing development support for 3D Design for HNTB's 33 design offices throughout the country.

Mr. Miguel is a registered architect for the state of Massachusetts and is a member of the American Institute of Architecture, the National Council of the Architectural Registration Boards, the Boston Society of Architects, the 3D Studio User's Group of Boston, and the North American Autodesk User's Group. His 3D computer models were featured in *Computer Graphics World*. He holds advanced degrees in architecture from Washington University in St. Louis, and the Massachusetts Institute of Technology (M.I.T.) in Cambridge, Massachusetts.

Chapter Overview

This chapter takes a look at exterior architectural models used in creating photorealistic still images. Issues regarding exterior models will include the types of 3D models, examples of exterior materials that were used for an actual project that used 3D design from preliminaries to final presentation, and rendered views of daytime views and nighttime views. Exercises in this chapter demonstrate using AutoCAD Release 13's feature of importing cameras from AutoCAD to 3D Studio, and using 3D Studio to create a fly-by over a large complex.

Exteriors of 3D Studio Meshes

Exterior models refer to 3D Studio meshes or models constructed to use for exterior viewing, such as architectural buildings, roads and highways, airports, or even entire cities. As such, these models are intended to serve the same role as the traditional physical scale-down constructed model. The computer model offers an advantage over the physically built model: the capabilities to realistically visualize how the proposed structures look in static still images and to walk through or fly by the proposed structures.

When you construct these exterior models, you need to decide on what to build, and more importantly, how detailed it needs to be for the purposes of your design. The problem with designing and constructing in a CAD program, such as AutoCAD, derives from the fact of just how exact (down to decimals or fractions of an inch) the program enables you to be. Architects and engineers do require that amount of precision in the construction drawings, so when they construct 3D models, they tend to create every single object in great detail. Yet for a typical perspective camera view of an entire building, taken many hundreds of feet away, you never see the texture or pattern of an exterior material unless you happen to zoom in for a closeup shot.

For an example of intricate details and their views from different distances, look at figures 4.1 and 4.2. This is a 3D model of a single bay at 22'-0" column-to-column for the new terminal building at T.F. Green Airport in Warwick, Rhode Island. The model was simulating a mock-up model usually built at the construction site, built to study the appearance of the custom frit pattern in the glazing system. The frit pattern consists of tiny 1-inch squares spaced about 1/2-inch apart, with a selected custom color.

The model was built in AutoCAD and brought into 3D Studio for rendering. The frit pattern shown was also drawn in AutoCAD, with each 1-inch square frit drawn as a closed polygon, arrayed accordingly, and brought into 3D Studio, where every single frit became a face. The glazing was assigned a green/blue glass material that was created in the Materials Editor, and the frit was assigned the custom color. All other objects (the column enclosures, the steel columns, and the mullions) remain the default material in 3D Studio.

Figure 4.2
*Closeup of frit pattern on
glazing. (Courtesy HNTB
Corp.)*

Figure 4.1 shows a rendered view of the bay at eye level on the departure level (the 2nd floor). This was to show what the effect of the frit pattern would look like. Depending on the type of resolution the final rendered image, the frit pattern may be visible. But not until you zoom in closely at the glazing (see fig. 4.2) can you tell that the frit is composed of tiny squares.

If this frit pattern created in AutoCAD was used for the glazing in the entire airport terminal building (see fig. 4.3), the file size would be tremendous due to the number of elements that the frit pattern would be composed of. Instead of creating each individual frit, a better method is to create materials in the Materials Editor that use an image of the frit pattern, and use the image as a map for the created material. (See the later section, "Signage and Lettering.")

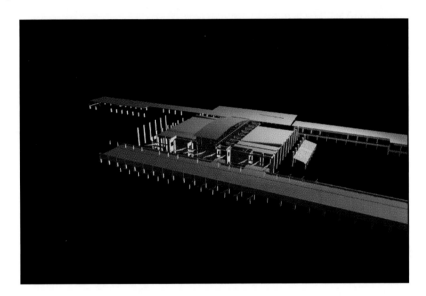

Figure 4.3

Aerial view of preliminary model of T.F. Green Airport. (Courtesy HNTB Corp.)

Constructing Exterior 3D Models

Architects generally show 3D representations of their design by building physical models. The types of models range from massing models built inexpensively of simple solid blocks, to intricate and highly detailed presentation models representing the types of materials the building is constructed of—and usually at a cost that can equal a price of an expensive sports car.

Similarly, in building a 3D model using a computer, the types of models can range from low-detail massing models to high-detail presentation models. The difference in these models is in the amount of detail created as objects; the more details used, the larger the number of objects, and the bigger the file sizes become. You need to use discretion in determining what needs to be built and how much detailing will show up in the final images or animation.

Figures 4.4 through 4.6 offer a comparison between a low-detail massing model and a high-detail presentation model. Figure 4.4 shows the rendered image of the OLDCITY.3DS file from the \3DS4\MESHES directory, and figure 4.5 shows the rendered image of PCACITY.3DS from the World Creating Toolkit Releases 3 & 4 in the \GEOMETRY\SCENES subdirectory. Figure 4.6 shows the status information for these two files, after rendering the Camera view to an 800×600 resolution. Note the differences between the number of faces, the number of vertices, the rendering time, and the swap file size; these are typical differences between low-detail massing models and high-detail presentation models.

Figure 4.4
*Aerial view of
OLDCITY.3DS,
a low-detail massing
model.*

3D Studio Architectural Rendering

Figure 4.6
The current status of
OLDCITY.3DS on the left,
and PCACITY.3DS on the
right. Note the differences
in the number of faces, the
number of vertices, the
rendering time, and the
swap file size.

Choosing Materials for Exterior Models

Choosing and selecting the materials to use is your most critical aspect for creating a realistic impression of the proposed design. Models made of stone, glass, plastic, or steel need to convey that appearance and characteristics of the given materials. Understanding and knowing the properties of certain materials is critical for mastering the ability to create photorealistic images. The Materials Editor enables you to obtain materials from the default 3DS library or manipulate them to create new materials. In addition, there are literally thousands of textures in 3D Studio's World Creating Toolkit, plus hundreds of aftermarket CD-ROMS with textures.

Invest in a good viewer, such as EYEBROWSER, to quickly view these textures. Certain aftermarket texture CD-ROMs come with illustrations of the texture images for a quick reference. There is also a German book called the *World Creating Toolkit* that has all the images and textures in 3D Studio's World Creating Toolkit, making it easier to view and locate images quickly.

To simplify material types, there are two basic types of materials to model buildings:

- ◆ Solid, such as brick, stone, concrete, steel, with matte or shiny matte that have no transparency.

- ◆ Transparent, such as glass for windows and glazed curtain wall systems, with clear or colored, shininess, and reflective.

You can take most materials you would need for a given 3D model directly from the 3DS materials library, the World Creating Toolkit, or other CD-ROMs with textures. For the most part, however, especially for architectural projects, you will end up creating your own custom materials not found anywhere else. You can revise characteristics of existing brick materials from the

3DS materials library (such as color and texture) to create variations of custom brick materials. For each project, it is wise to create a separate materials library file (*.MLI) rather than loading new materials into the existing default 3DS.MLI library file.

If you want to create unique materials, however, the best method is to scan the actual sample of the material, or preferably, take a photograph of a mock-up sample wall to use as mapping. Figure 4.7 shows a photograph of an actual mock-up wall of the Arriscraft material built for the Northeastern University Recreation Center. Several types of mock-up walls were built, using different exterior materials such as brown brick, white brick, concrete block, and the Arriscraft (chosen material), to study and determine which material to use for the actual building. Because the sample wall was not available during the design phase, I had to create the material using some of the default materials as a start, and change their properties, such as using different texture maps, adjusting color, or adjusting the lighting properties.

Figure 4.7

Photograph of Arriscraft from sample mock-up wall, Northeastern University.

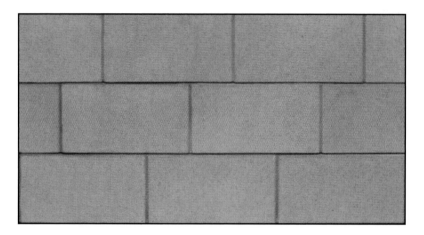

 **NOTE**

Photographs of materials can be revised in an image-editing program, such as Aldus Photostyler or Adobe Photoshop, to correct contrast, adjust brightness, or correct position of joints of the masonry work due to parallax created from the camera tilting. Problems with tiling may occur when using images as maps for materials. An excellent tutorial on tiling maps is included in *Inside 3D Studio Release 4* by New Riders Publishing.

Masonry

Figure 4.8 shows the view of the recreation center from across the street. This camera view shows the entire building plus the surrounding site. The primary attribute of the masonry from this distance is its color; subtle textures of the masonry are not apparent. Compare them with a view close to the building, as shown in figure 4.9, and the textures become more apparent. If you study photographs of architectural buildings, you will notice that textures are hard to see in a distant shot unless the masonry is heavily rusticated.

Figure 4.8
Perspective view of Northeastern University Marino Recreation Center. (Courtesy HNTB Corp.)

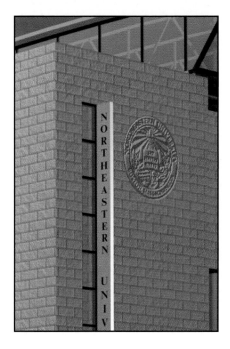

Figure 4.9
Closeup view of east wall. (Courtesy HNTB Corp.)

Glazing

Creating glass material could be simple if all you needed to do was to use the default materials. Unfortunately, in the real architectural world, there are a myriad of glass types, consisting of colors, tints, reflective coatings, and as previously mentioned, ceramic frit patterns within the glazing.

For an interior view of the building, using the default glass types, such as clear glass, may be adequate to show a background through the glass, such as the sky. For an exterior shot, however, there are difficult parameters. For a daytime view of the building, the color of the glazing may be difficult to see due to the glass reflecting the blue sky, for instance. Reflections of surrounding elements, such as trees or neighboring buildings, will also cast a reflection. Finally, there is the effect of sunlight, creating highlights, shadows, and reflections.

Figure 4.10 shows a closeup detail of the glazing system used for the Northeastern University Recreation Center. The glass material was created using the default green glass, adjusted to a blue-green tint, with the reflective map in the Materials Editor set to Automatic with the flat mirror option. Reflections of the steel columns are visible in the glazing.

Figure 4.10

View of glazing and steel column, Northeastern University. (Courtesy HNTB Corp.)

3D Studio Architectural Rendering

You can change the characteristics of color, reflectivity, and shininess of glass materials from the 3DS library to create diverse glass materials. To create a reflective curtain wall with a mirror finish, for example, you would have to set the reflective map type to Automatic with the flat mirror turned on. Note that any type of reflective properties, such as reflective glass, increases the rendering time owing to the extensive computations 3D Studio (or AutoCAD) must perform to mirror the image, as well as calculate light turned on and shadows cast.

Signage and Lettering

Figures 4.11 and 4.12 illustrate two other options that were studied for the east wall. These studies were done for design options of identifying the building to the university, showing the name and the seal of the university. One proposal was for a metal seal, whereas the other was carved into stone.

Figure 4.11
Metal university seal at the east wall. (Courtesy HNTB Corp.)

Figure 4.12
Cast-stone seal at the east wall. (Courtesy HNTB Corp.)

For both of the seals, a scanned image of the Northeastern University logo was used as a map. In the Materials Editor of 3D Studio, the metal logo used an opacity map to allow the open areas to be transparent. The cast-stone look was achieved by using the Bump map set to Reverse. It may have been possible to actually build the model of the metal logo, but using this mapped method reduces the object to a single element versus an object composed of thousands of faces and elements to make up the metal logo.

The lettering was created in the 2D Shaper and 3D Lofter, and inserted into place at the east wall as well as the top glazing of the curved curtain wall. Here again, I could have chosen the option of using materials with mapped images in the Materials Editor to save file size.

Paint Color Variations

As well as working with materials, using the Materials Editor to assign different types of colored material to a 3D object enables the architect to study various color schemes. Figure 4.13 shows four different color studies of the roadway canopies for T.F. Green Airport.

Figure 4.13

Four color studies of the roadway canopies for T.F. Green Airport. (Courtesy HNTB Corp.)

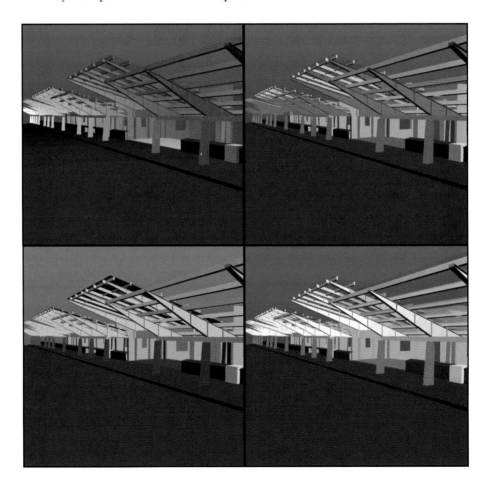

3D Objects Used and Hidden in Exterior Views

To cut down on rendering time, you should hide objects that aren't visible for the particular image. If you have a model constructed of interior and exterior objects but must render only the exterior for a daytime scene, for example, you should use the Display/Hide command to hide objects not to be seen. Naming objects appropriately to allow for hiding objects, therefore, assumes great importance.

Refer back to figure 4.8 for a daytime view of the building. The interiors of the recreation center are slightly visible, such as the roof trusses plus some walls and columns. Yet there are more objects in the interior view of the building. Figure 4.14 shows an interior view of the gymnasium level with all the interior elements visible. For the most part, the majority of the interior elements, such as the floor, carpet, base trim work, doors, and some railing should be hidden using Display/Hide and selecting objects not visible for an exterior daytime shot.

Figure 4.14

Interior view of multipurpose room, Northeastern University. (Courtesy HNTB Corp.)

You might need to leave the interior objects on for a nighttime view, however, because with the lights turned on inside the building, the interiors often are visible from the outside. Figure 4.15 illustrates a night view of a student recreation center, in which the interiors are visible owing to the light source within the building.

Deciding Which Objects Should Be Visible

Regarding building the model, you should always keep in mind that sometimes you can get carried away building every part of the 3D model, from the smallest detail visible in the interiors to the detail of a blade of grass. Unless you do heavy Hollywood-type animation in which your storyboard shows a minute detail of the texture of the brick material zooming out to an aerial view of a particular building, you really don't need to try to show everything that won't be visible throughout the duration of the animation.

The opposite applies to still images, however, because you need to show every detail pertaining to the particular view, created for a high-resolution image. A client might not notice certain subtleties while viewing an animation on the monitor or through a videotape, yet if that client has a hard copy still image of say, an 8×10 color photograph, he or she could notice every finite detail of the image. Architects dealing with the material choices and color selections especially must consider this issue, and the models they construct usually require a high degree of detail.

Figures 4.16 through 4.18 show a proposed pavilion at T.F. Green Airport in Warwick, Rhode Island, designed to allow departing passengers to get from the ground-level parking lot up to the departure level on the second floor. Inside, there is an escalator, a stair, and an elevator for access to the departure level. The intricate guardrails consist of stainless steel rods spaced 2-1/2 inches apart. For the still image, small detailing such as the guardrail will be visible. For the animation through the pavilion, the guardrail would just appear as a blur in the background. The guardrail could have been replaced by a material with a map applied, just like the signs mentioned in the previous section.

Figure 4.16
*Exterior view of stair pavil-
ion, T.F. Green Airport.
(Courtesy HNTB Corp.)*

Figure 4.17
*Interior view of stair pavil-
ion, T.F. Green Airport.
(Courtesy HNTB Corp.)*

Using Appropriate Materials for Different Distances

Depending on the distance of the camera views and the path of the anima-tion, you might have to use various materials for the same object depending on the view of the building. Still images might require that you use a material you produce by using texture mapped photographic images to show realism. But if the entire sequence of an animation is of an aerial view from a certain distance, you really don't need to use the same detailed material when a simi-lar material of the same color would suffice. If the animation passes the mater-ial quickly, the resulting animation might appear to be a blur in which the finite details don't even show. If you don't have time to change materials back and forth between the fine detailed material and the simpler material, stick with the detailed material. If your goal is to save time because you need to generate several animation renderings and must cut down rendering time, however, then go for the appropriate models for the required rendering purpose.

TIP

Keep a single master model as the base, and copy several models with vari-ous material types from the close-up, detailed version to the model used for far shots. Imagine Hollywood movie setups creating various movie sets for different scenes.

Setting Up Camera Views for Still Images

3D Studio offers a powerful, easy-to-use camera feature that behaves similarly to an actual 35 mm single lens reflex camera. The 3D Studio camera acts similarly to the AutoCAD camera, yet also operates at a higher level in the following ways:

- ◆ Offers far greater control over the distance and type of lens

- ◆ Offers more powerful capability to calculate field of vision

- ◆ Offers better dollying capabilities

- ◆ Illustrates more clearly the location of the camera and its target on-screen

To generate realistic camera views, you should understand some basic photographic knowledge. You don't have to be a professional photographer to use 3D Studio's camera, but understanding types of lens, field of vision, effects using wide angle and zoom lens, and target viewpoint, helps you be able to create some photorealistic images without coming off like an amateur.

Recording Photographs of the Existing Site

When you take photographs of an existing site to use as backgrounds for 3D Studio models, you should note the date and time of the photographs, plus the type of camera and lens you use (for example, 35 mm versus a 4×5, 28 mm versus 50 mm). Location on the site would also be beneficial for creating camera views in AutoCAD using the DVIEW command, for which the cameras can be imported to 3D Studio. Noting the date and the time of the year also lets you use AutoVision to create the light source for importing into 3D Studio.

Matching Camera View from AutoCAD DVIEW Perspective Views

In AutoCAD Release 12 or earlier, you couldn't import camera perspective views created with the Dview command into 3D Studio using the DXFOUT command To re-create camera views, you first had to jot down the location of the target and the camera, the camera zoom lens used, and the height ("z" coordinate). Next, you had to create a line with a thickness or a 3D face from the target point to the camera point, and then you had to try to create the camera using this line or face imported into 3D Studio as a guide for camera and target placement.

AutoCAD Release 13's 3DSOUT command eliminates this problem. Perspective views you use the Dview command to create and save as views convert to 3D Studio cameras with the same corresponding view names as the camera names.

Using the SITE-3D.DWG of the house in Chapter 1, the following is an quick exercise in importing the cameras from AutoCAD Release 13 into 3D Studio Release 4. Open the SITE-3D.DWG model used from Chapter 1 and save it as SITE-3DW.DWG. If you haven't done the exercise from Chapter 1, do the following exercise to create the PER-1 Camera view, otherwise skip to the exercise after that.

Start AutoCAD Release 13, and open SITE-3D.DWG from the AutoCAD Release 12 ACAD or ACADWIN \sample subdirectory. If you do not have this AutoCAD file, use the NAYLOR.3DS file in the World Creating Toolkit under /Geometry/Architex and import the 3DS file to AutoCAD Release 13.

Creating Camera Views in AutoCAD Release 13

Command: **Tilemode**	Issues the Tilemode
New Value for TILEMODE<0>: **1** Regenerating drawing	Converts to Modelspace view
Command: **Plan** <Current UCS>/Ucs/World: Press Enter	Issues the PLAN VIEW command
Command: **Zoom** All/Center/Dynamic/Extents/ Left/Previous/Vmax/Window/ <Scale(X/XP)>: **W**	Issues the ZOOM command Zooms window to enlarge the house view
Command: **Dview**	Issues the DVIEW command
Select objects: **W**	Issues window option for selecting objects
First corner: Pick top left corner	Selects the house
Other corner: Pick bottom right corner	
Select objects: Press Enter	Completes selection
CAmera/TArget/Distance/POints /PAn/Zoom/Twist/Clip/Hide/Off /Undo/<eXit>: **PO**	Selects POints option
Enter Target point <...>: **.XY** of Pick center of house	Target point at center of house
Need Z: **5'6"**	Target height

```
Enter Camera point <..>: .XY
of Pick point to south east part
```
See figure 4.19 for Camera position

See figure 4.19 for Camera position

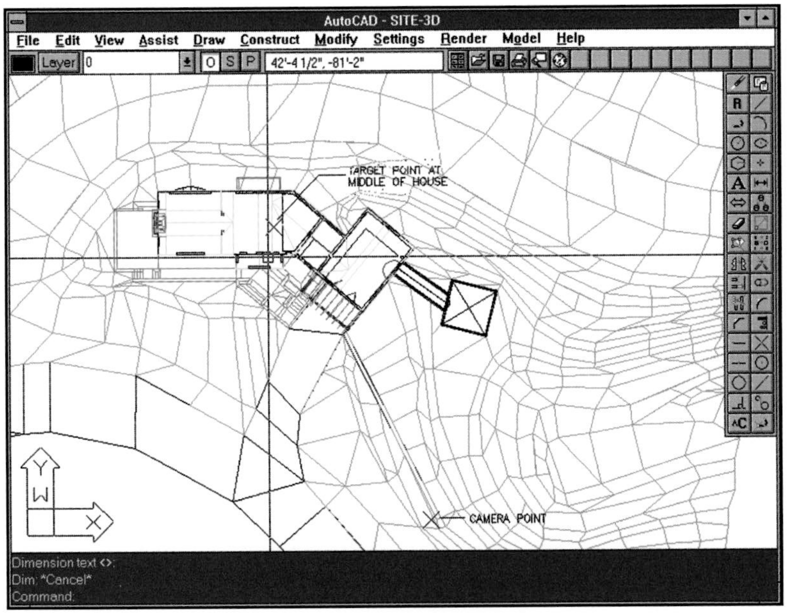

Figure 4.19

Camera and target positions for house.

```
Need Z: 5'6"
```

```
CAmera/TArget/Distance/POints
/PAn/Zoom/Twist/Clip/Hide/Off
/Undo/<eXit>: D
```
Issues DISTANCE command to go to perspective mode

```
New Camera/Target distance<..>: 90
```
Enters distance around 90'

```
CAmera/TArget/Distance/POints
/PAn/Zoom/Twist/Clip/Hide/Off
/Undo/<eXit>: H
```
Hides lines to see image

View of the House is zoomed too close. Adjust the camera lens from 50 mm (default) to 30 mm wide angle lens.

```
CAmera/TArget/Distance/POints
/PAn/Zoom/Twist/Clip/Hide/Off
/Undo/<eXit>: Z
```
Issues the ZOOM lens command

```
Adjust lens length <50 mm>: 30
```
Zooms to 30 mm lens

```
CAmera/TArget/Distance/POints
/PAn/Zoom/Twist/Clip/Hide/Off
/Undo/<eXit>: Press Enter
```
Exits DVIEW command

```
Command: View
```
Issues the VIEW command

```
?/Delete/Restore/Save/Window: S
View name to save: PER-1
```
Saves the view as PER-1

To see the house with the hidden lines removed, use the HIDE command or the SHADE command with SHADEDGE set to 2 for lines.

Figure 4.20 illustrates what should appear on-screen. Click on the perspective view to activate it.

Figure 4.20

SITE-3D.DWG with perspective, isometric, and elevation views.

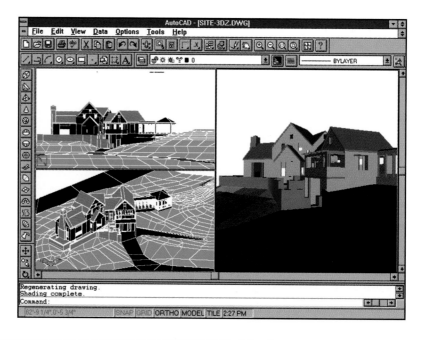

3DSOUT Command in AutoCAD Release 13

Command: **UCS**	Issues the UCS command
Origin/ZAxis/3Point/OBject/ View/X/Y/Z/Prev/Restore/Save/ Del/?/<World>: Press Enter	Restores UCS to world
Command: **3DSOUT**	Issues the 3DSOUT command
Initializing ...	
Initializing Render ...	
Select objects: **ALL**	Selects all objects
1347 found:	
Select objects: Press Enter	

The 3D Studio Output file appears. Save the file as SITE-3DW.3DS (note directory to which you save it—it should be in the C:\R13\WIN\SAMPLE directory or wherever the SITE-3DW.DWG file is located). Next, the 3D Studio File

Export Options dialog box appears (see fig. 4.21). Enable the Layer radio button option in the Derive 3D Studio Objects From area, accept the defaults for the rest, and click on OK.

Figure 4.21
The 3D Studio File Export Options dialog box.

Save and quit AutoCAD Release 13, and start up 3D Studio.

1. Load the SITE-3DW.3DS file you just created in AutoCAD Release 13. Click on the lower left viewport, type **C** to activate the Camera view, and the PER-1 view should appear (see fig. 4.22).

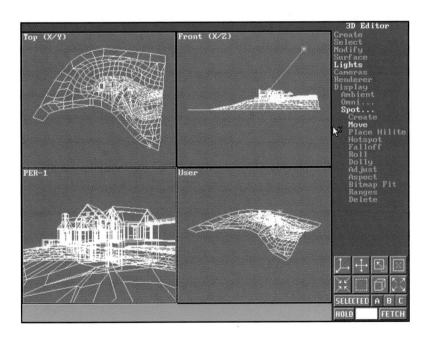

Figure 4.22
Spotlight location for 3D house.

2. Choose Lights/Spotlight/Create. Create a spotlight for the view, then move the light up for a mid-afternoon view. Adjust the cone to cover the entire site (see fig. 4.23).

Figure 4.23

*View of screen in 3D
Studio of SITE-3DW.3DS,
with Camera view
activated.*

3. Click on the single viewport button to make the PER-1 viewport the full screen. Choose Program/CAMERA PREVU (or press F7) to get into the 3D Editor Camera Control and Match Perspective. This allows for a quicker preview rendering than using the Render/Render View command.

4. Click on the Backgrnd button and select SKY.JPG from the C:\3DS4\MAPS subdirectory (see fig. 4.24).

Figure 4.24

*Perspective rendering in
CAMERA PREVU.*

5. Exit the CAMERA PREVU and select the vports button to display the four viewports. Choose Camera/Adjust and click in the PER-1 viewport to see the Camera controls for Camera PER-1.

Note that the camera lens has changed from the 30 mm lens setting from AutoCAD Release 13, perhaps owing to the amount of accuracy in decimal points between the AutoCAD setting and the 3D Studio setting. The viewing angle of the perspective view remains identical, but you should set the camera settings in AutoCAD regarding the camera and target points to whole numbers if possible.

Figure 4.25 illustrates an AutoCAD image of the house rendered with hidden lines removed using the HIDE command, superimposed with a rendered 3D Studio image. The two images were brought into Aldus Photostyler, with the 3D Studio image cropped and superimposed over the AutoCAD image. This illustrates a technique trying to highlight a certain part of a building.

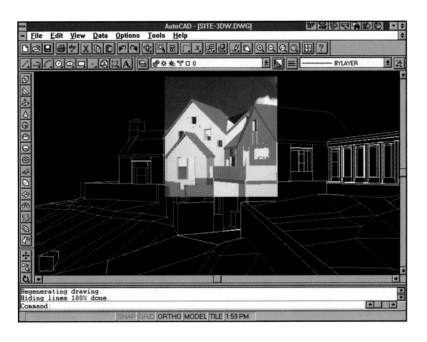

Figure 4.25
AutoCAD hidden-line view with rendered 3D Studio image.

Using 3D Studio Camera Controls in 3D Editor

Using the Camera feature in 3D Studio is fairly straightforward. The camera simulates a standard 35 mm SLR camera. You just choose Camera/Create to create a camera, set a target point and the camera location, and select the appropriate settings in the Camera Definition dialog box. The Camera dialog box is important for matching the 3D model with a photograph.

> **Having the information of camera type, lens type, as well as approximate camera location, height, and target helps when you try to match the background to the 3D model.**

One problem you face when you create cameras in 3D Studio is the lack of precise camera location. If you originally generate the 3D model in AutoCAD and import it into 3D Studio, you can use the 3DSOUT in AutoCAD Release 13 for precise location, as shown in the previous exercise.

When you want to create photorealistic camera views, you must consider the use of the 3D Studio camera as a real 35 mm camera. You don't need to study photojournalism or know darkroom techniques. Having a basic understanding of using a real 35 mm camera will help you in using the 3D Studio camera. Understand what using a super-wide angle lens or a telephoto or zoom lens will do to your scene. Know how the field of vision effects the appearance of the view, and how views outside of the cone of vision become severely distorted.

Perspective Matching: 3D Studio Release 4

3D Studio Release 4 furnishes a feature that enables you to do perspective matching easily and more accurately using the photographic image as a background for the 3D model or mesh. Chapter 2, "Camera Control and Match Perspective," of *Autodesk 3D Studio Release 4 New Features*, offers a very good tutorial for learning and using this perspective matching feature.

Two examples of 3D models superimposed with a photographic background are shown in figures 4.26 and 4.27. Figure 4.26 shows an aerial view of Boston, with an exterior massing model of the recreation center near the center of the image (see blow up). Figure 4.27 shows the view of the recreation center at street level, with the model of building set on the site. For both images, I had to use an image-editing software program such as Aldus Photostyler for correct foreground figures, such as the existing buildings in front of the aerial view and the cars for the street level view.

Figure 4.26

Aerial view of Boston, with closeup of recreation center. (Courtesy HNTB Corp.)

Figure 4.26
Continued

Figure 4.27
*Street-level view of
Northeastern University
Marino Recreation Center.
(Courtesy HNTB Corp.)*

Rendering for High-Resolution Images

After you create the views (the cameras and the light setups are created), final output to a hard copy requires some additional steps. Time and again, people ask me how to generate some really high resolution color hard copies, usually

8×10 photographic images, for presentation or distribution to clients. Many different types of color printers exist in today's market, ranging from very affordable bubblejet printers to expensive offset color printers used for high-end publications. You should research several copy places and service bureaus to find out what type of high-resolution color printers they have, what resolution (dots per inches or pixels per inch) they can generate, and finally the cost of printing.

Color images on your video monitor appear to be high resolution, with images typically shown in 640×480 or 1024×768, depending on your monitor size. Yet, when you send these same images out for final images, that on-screen crispness disappears. It used to be that you needed to render the images at a higher number of pixels than the typical computer monitor resolution, with the belief that screen resolutions matching process resolutions will yield good results This is no longer true. 1600×1200 will provide excellent results in 8×10 glossies, and 1024×768 or 1280×1024 (common screen resolutions) will produce nice results in modern processes which antialias nonintegral dpi counts, such as most current dyesub and photoimagery processes. Furthermore, a service bureau that insists on using TIFs or TGAs with imbedded dpi counts is no better than a service bureau that can't read a standard TIF WITHOUT embedded dpi information—which Photoshop and other programs will interpret as being in INCHES across a figure equal to the resolution

STOP

Remember to set the rendering to "Null" rather than your default settings, (RDPADI or VIBRANT); otherwise, the current video settings override any higher image settings (see fig. 4.28). I made this mistake several times in the beginning before figuring out what happened. (And only then from advice from fellow 3D Studio users—that's what I get for not reading the 3D Studio manuals or New Riders books.)

Figure 4.28
Rendering device
configuration.

Sun Positioning

A particularly effective type of animation is to create the effect of time-lapse photography, in which a still camera records a view of the exterior 3D model, and shows the light and shadows cast by the building during the course of a particular day.

Using Autodesk's AutoVision's Sun Locator feature would prove beneficial. AutoVision, which runs inside AutoCAD, lets you create the position of the sunlight for any location in the world. The Geographical locator lets you pin-point locations of major cities throughout the world by selecting the list cities, clicking on the maps of all the continents, or even entering the latitude and longitude of a particular location. For a given date and time of day, a light is created, and repeating the process for various times of the same day will provide for several positions of the sun. Exporting the AutoCAD file as a 3DS file in AutoCAD Release 13, 3D Studio then takes those lights and converts them into it into spotlights, which you can use to create a path for the movement of the sun.

There is also a sun positioning plug-in for 3D Studio called the SOLAR-TRACK IPAS (available from the Pyros Partnership). This program charts a path of the sun's position relative to the selected object given the specific date, location, and duration. Applying a spotlight to the path in the Keyframer will resulted in an arced path of the sun during a given date.

Note

Drive-Bys and Fly-Bys

Constructing the model is by far the most time-consuming part, from the time you create a 3D model to finally rendering animation, compared to creating still images and animating the completed exterior model. Models of buildings, cities, bridges, or landscapes usually don't involve moving objects, so the animation to illustrate the design intent usually consists of the camera moving over and through the 3D model. Because of the size of the 3D model as exterior models, animating them usually is associated with views from a moving automobile or from a flying structure such as a helicopter or a plane.

The Moving Camera

The moving camera used in animation is more like a motion picture camera. Think of a moving camera as a flying object, such as a plane, that flies through the model and records the flight through its camera. You have to create the flight path for the camera to fly, and you want to make that path as fluid as the flight path of a plane. Any sharp, quick turn of the camera results in a blurring effect—imagine using a camcorder recording everything without shutting off the recording while you turn quickly to shoot various views.

Developing a Storyboard

You really need to create a storyboard if you want to produce effective computer animation. 3D Studio users can create some animation while playing with 3D Studio, but effectively conveying your message and intentions to others requires a set of strong ideas put down into sketch form so you can produce some successful animation.

You might study books on cartoon animation and film making, for example. These books show you that artists draw up very rough sketches illustrating scenes throughout a movie; that's *storyboarding*. (Figure 4.29 shows an example of storyboarding.) Or, you might study movies and film. As you watch a movie, pretend you're the director and imagine how you need to compose the shots, the views, and the sequence. The ultimate goal is to tell a good story, because all the special effects are wasted if they don't contribute effectively to telling the story. Although your animation might not be as sophisticated, nevertheless, deciding on what and how the animation should appear instead of going full speed without a plan is important.

Figure 4.29

Storyboard sketch of animation for Northeastern University.

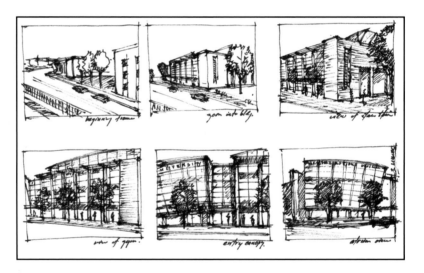

NOTE

I recently saw an animation generated by a user taking a very long path through a proposed convention center. You sat at a computer and using the mouse, took a walk through the 3D model, encountering every section of the convention. This method is effective for interactive use, where the user wants to take a tour of the 3D model. But as a storyteller, the long trip through the convention suffered from the lack of effective storyboarding, and needed editing. It was as if someone turned on the video camcorder and recorded the walk through the entire convention center. Filmmakers do not just turn on the camera and shoot the entire movie in one long two-hour take. You have to be an effective storyteller by video-editing certain key scenes together and moving through the scene at key locations of interest, in order to make an effective animation that tells a good story.

Background Setup for the Fly-By

You have to use the sky as a background for daytime exterior animation, you can't just use the background method used for still image renderings. Because the camera moves through the site, the sky remains unchanged while the building viewpoint changes, which gives your animation a decidedly artificial appearance. You can approach this sky background problem from a couple different directions:

◆ Building a planetarium or a dome over the entire building or site. If the animation requires a moving camera, you want to build a huge megadome over the building (or preferably the city) to serve as the sky, and add the material sky texture or any other sky or clouds material to the inside surface of the dome. Choose Create/Hemisph to build the sky dome or planetarium over the building or city, then choose Surface/Normals/Object Flip to make sure that the inside rather than the outside of the dome is visible (see fig. 4.30). Be sure to delete the bottom of the hemisphere; otherwise, the sky will appear on the "ground." See figure 4.31 for the sky effect for the dome; see what happens when the bottom of the hemisphere is not deleted?

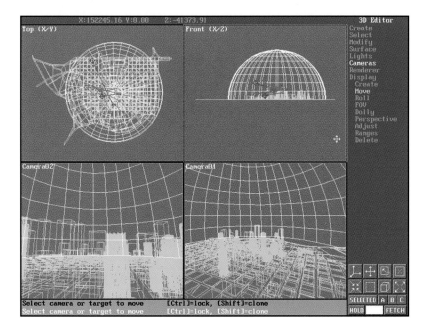

Figure 4.30

The planetarium or dome over the city in the 3D Editor.

◆ For an animation using a time-lapse still camera, you might need to use the movement of the clouds to illustrate the realism of a fast time-lapse photography. One way to achieve cloud movement, depending on the time-lapse of the animation, would be to map the sky texture material to a huge "billboard" and move it slightly, rotating the sky dome. Another way might be to use Animator Studio to create a 2D animation of the moving clouds, or to capture a video of a time-lapse movement of the clouds.

Project: Fly-By of the Parliament Building of Canberra

The Parliament House in Canberra, Australia, was a 1980 competition winning scheme by the architectural firm of Mitchell Giurgola of New York. For this fly-by exercise, you use the 3DS model of this building in the World Creating Toolkit, and generate an animation from high up in the air of flying down and circling the parliament building, and finally landing on the site.

1. Start 3D Studio, choose File/Load, and load the file PARLEMNT.3DS (located in the \GEOMETRY\ARCHITEX\ subdirectory) from the World Creating Toolkit Releases 3 & 4. CD-ROM (see fig. 4.32). Press Alt+C and Alt+L to make the camera and light visible. Click in the Top viewport to make it current.

Note that the file consists of 59 objects made of materials that are representative of the colors from AutoCAD, and that no mapped materials are present.

2. Go to the 2D Shaper and choose Display/3D Display/Choose. Click on All and click on OK. Choose Display/3D Display/On and use the Zoom windows button to zoom in to the 3D model (see fig. 4.33).

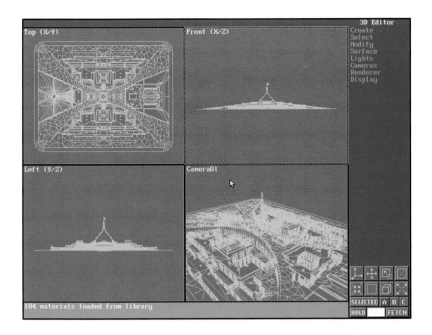

Figure 4.32
PARLEMNT.3DS from the World Creating Toolkit, in the 3D Editor.

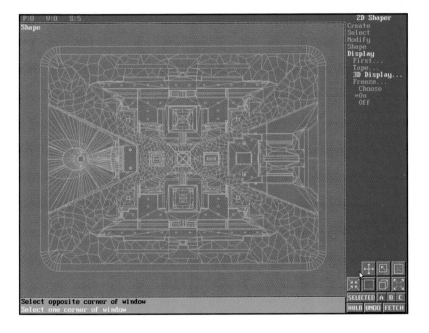

Figure 4.33
Top view in the 2D Shaper.

3. Choose Create/Line and draw a series of 9 line segments that starts at the lower left corner of the site; circles clockwise around the site; and ends at the front court, circular court at 9 o'clock to the central flag mast (see fig. 4.34).

Figure 4.34

Straight line path in the Shaper.

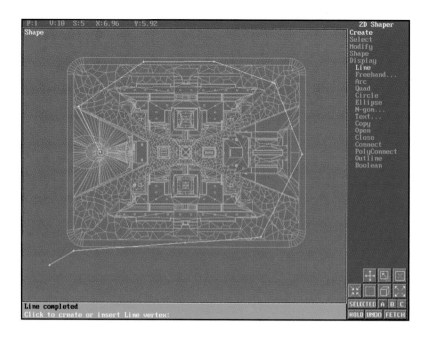

4. Choose Modify/Polygon/Curve and select the polygon you just drew. Modify the polygon by choosing Modify/Vertex/Move and Modify/Vertex/Adjust, and pressing and holding down the pick button to adjust the spline curves (see fig. 4.35).

Figure 4.35

Adjusted path to a curve with spline adjustment.

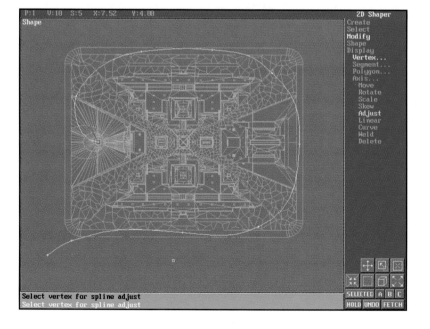

3D Studio Architectural Rendering

5. Choose Program/3D Lofter or press F2 to go to the Lofter, and choose Path/Get/Shaper. Click on OK when the "Replace the current path" dialog box appears. Choose Path/Steps and set the path steps down to zero, then click on OK.

6. Choose 3D Display/Choose, and select Flag*, Frontco*, and mastf01 and click on OK. Choose 3D Display/On, and the objects you selected appear on-screen.

For this animation, the camera starts up high looking toward the flag mast and gradually descends and lands on the court. You need to bring up the vertices of the path brought in accordingly.

7. Choose Views/Drawing Aids and set the snap spacing in the x: column to .05, click on the Y: adjacent to the X: column to change the Y: and z:, and click on OK. Press the S key to activate the Snap mode. Click on the Front viewport to activate it, and move up each of the vertices up the z direction by choosing Path/Move Vertex, and hit the Tab key until the arrows are vertical, starting with the first vertex at the lower left corner. (See table 4.1.)

TIP

Enlarge the Front viewport, and if necessary, turn off the 3D Display. If you select the wrong vertices, right-click to cancel the command.

Table 4.1   Distance Vertices To Be Moved in the Z Direction

Vertex	Moved Up in Z Direction
1	2.5
2	1.25
3	.5
4	.4
5	.3
6	.2
7	.2
8	.15
9	.05
10	0

8. Choose Path/Steps and set the number of sets to 10 (see figs. 4.36 and 4.37).

Figure 4.36

Path with vertices moved in the 3D Lofter.

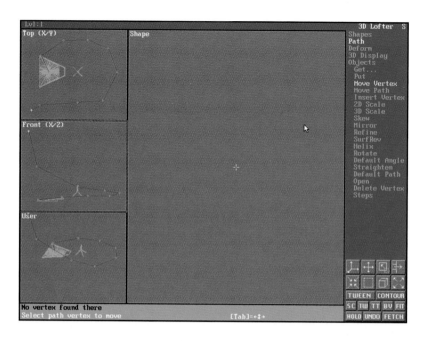

Figure 4.37

Front view of path after steps to 10.

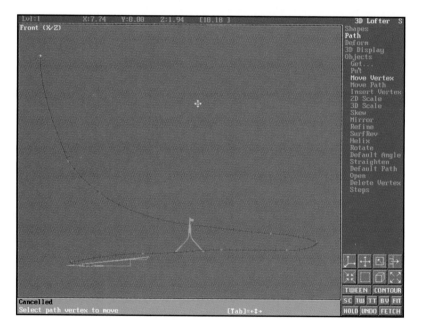

Having now created the path, you're ready to import it into the Keyframer. Upon closer examination, you can see that the *end of the path* is landing right at the base of the building, so you should raise the entire path slightly to around eye level or higher.

9. Maximize the front view, and zoom in to the last vertex. Turn off Snap by pressing S, choose Path/Move Path, click on the path, and move it up the z direction around .04 units.

10. Choose Program/3D Editor or press the F3 key, and make a copy of Camera01 by choosing Cameras/Move, press and hold down Ctrl+Shift, select Camera01, and Move/Clone the camera to the lower left corner of the site, accepting the name of the new camera as Camera02. Move the Camera02 target to the flag and mast. Click on the lower right viewport with the Camera01 view, press C, select Camera02, and click on OK.

11. Choose Program/Keyframer or press the F4 key, then choose Time/Segment and set the number of frames to 330. Choose Paths/ Get/Lofter and select Camera02 to apply the path. When the Get Path dialog box appears, click on the following buttons:

    Relocate object to path start? **yes**

    Reverse path direction? **no**

    Adjust key for constant speed? **yes**

    Click on OK.

12. Choose Paths/Show-Hide and click on Camera02 in any viewport, or use the H key to see the names of all objects (see fig. 4.38).

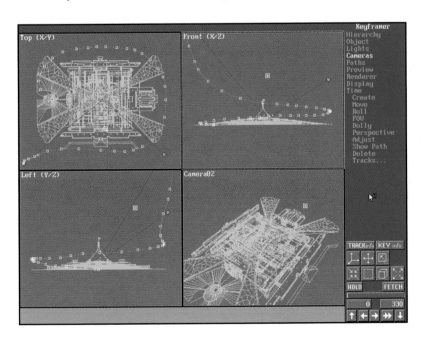

Figure 4.38
Path for Camera02 from the 3D Lofter to the Keyframer.

13. Move the slider bar at the bottom to see the view of the animation from Camera02, or press the play (double arrow) button to see the animation. For a quick preview, choose Preview/Make to review the animation (see figs. 4.39 and 4.40).

Figure 4.39
Start of animation of Camera02.

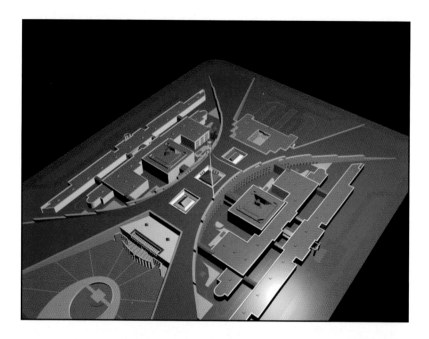

Figure 4.40
Camera02 at frame 120.

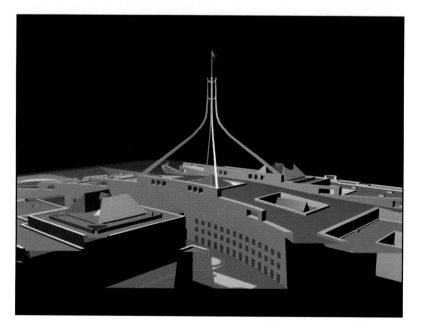

You have created a simple fly-thru animation that focuses on the central part of the Parliament Building, the flag mast. In typical architectural animation, this is the typical result required to convey the design intent.

If the view is a simulation of the pilot's view, however, do the same process as 3D Studio's tutorial for the walkthrough. Choose Hierarchy/Create Dummy and attach the path brought in from the 3D Lofter to the dummy object. Choose Camera/Create, create a camera and attach the target to the dummy object, or attach both the camera and the target to the flying dummy platform. Choose Paths/Follow to force the camera to align itself with the path. The animation should now show the camera view following a flight path, which could be much more exciting as an special effect of the flight or ride that you're taking than looking at the surroundings.

Summary

Creating successful exterior computer models depends on your skill in 3D design depending on which CAD system you use as well as using 3D Studio. Remember that the amount of detail necessary for viewing the model as a high-resolution still image will vary from viewing the model as part of an animation. Materials selection is the key in creating a realistic model, with lighting effects to make the materials in the objects look real, and using the camera to finalize the "real" image. Animation is the end product to produce the image of realism, but without realistic-looking models, the animation will be ineffective.

Practice these exercises, and do the tutorials, but ultimately, dare to experiment and explore and enjoy creating exterior models.

Lighting Day and Night

Chapter 5

Flores and Associates Architects, Principles: Tony Flores, Wayne C. Cully
By authorization of WRT Energy, Corporation

by Martha L. Rowlett

Houston, Texas

Author Bio

Martha L. Rowlett is a native Texan. She earned a bachelor's of science in environmental design from Texas A&M in 1978. Martha worked in architectural illustration and computer graphics for 17 years before starting her own firm in September 1995. Payne Rowlett specializes in architectural and engineering computer graphics.

Chapter Overview

Architectural illustrations are important to designers and builders, who use the renderings in their presentations to clients. Most people have a hard time looking at 2D plans and elevations and then visualizing a 3D structure from those plans. This is where architectural illustration comes into play—helping people see in 3D what the design looks like before anything is constructed. Architects have been using computers since the 1980s to help present ideas to clients in 2D, and now some firms even use 3D programs, such as 3D Studio, to help their clients through the architectural design process.

3D Studio is an amazing product that architects should use not only for their final renderings but throughout the whole design process. You can build geometric shapes, bring the shapes into 3D Studio, set up a perspective view, and create lighting for the model. From there, you can design your building in a 3D form, showing your client different stages of your model. Your client sees the design he is getting from the beginning of the project. When the building is better defined, materials can be placed on the object, and lighting can be placed in its exact location.

Because less time will be spent in the design process, using 3D Studio at the beginning of a project will reduce the amount of people needed to design the project and complete the presentation. Imagine: you can have infinite views of your building, eliminating the need for an expensive model. You can change a color or type of material on your building with a trip to the Materials Editor. Designers can use 3D Studio's lighting abilities to study certain interior lighting schemes or to show the different effects of exterior lighting on the materials of the building. 3D Studio has many uses in today's design world.

The Importance of Lighting in Illustrations

You use different lighting when setting any scene; night scenes, for example, require different color and intensity of lighting than a middle of the day shot. For all your renderings, you should not be content to use a few lights and render the final image. Lighting should be as important as any of the processing you go through to create a final rendering.

3D Studio provides the illustrator with many different types of lighting. A 3D Studio user will encounter many special lighting situations when dealing with architectural renderings. The project discussed in this chapter used different lighting setups to achieve each of the five views. Once you understand the lighting commands and how they work in 3D Studio, you can implement this knowledge into your models.

Architects can walk their clients through and around the building in animation. A building can be placed on a site with adjacent buildings to show their relationship in actual 3D. You can show the interaction of the building and different lighting during the day. The designer can go into an interior space and show the exact location of lights and how these lights and the exterior light will affect the ambiance of the room. You have endless possibilities when using 3D Studio for lighting. Creating realistic lighting is essential for making a still image of a building look real.

Many elements make up a good architectural illustration, and lighting is one of the most important. Lighting serves the following purposes in illustrations:

◆ Creates contrast between different planes of a building

◆ Produces different moods and effects in an illustration

◆ Indicates the time of day in the image

◆ Reveals and highlights the various materials that constitute the building

◆ Indicates the type and color of lighting in interior spaces

Project Overview

Project: WRT Energy Corporate Headquarters

Location: Houston, Texas

Architect: Flores and Associates Architects

Principles: Tony Flores and Wayne C. Cully

This job was a proposed office, condominium, and hotel in a wooded area near Houston.

We created five still shots enlarged to 30ʋ40 from color transparencies, plus a 1 minute, 20 second animation, in about four weeks. We rendered two aerials that we used as both the start and finish of part of the animation and one night scene, which we also included in the animation. In the animation, we substituted fireworks for the moon. For the final two illustrations, we used a dusk scene and an interior of the office building's lobby. We constructed the plans of buildings in 2D in Cadkey.

Usually by this stage, architects are lucky to have the building designed by the deadline. Because of our timeframe, we opted not to do certain things that would have enhanced the renderings, which was unfortunate. When you have a deadline, however, you often must make decisions that decrease rendering time, but that also affect the final output of the job.

We frequently decide the final result based specifically on the purpose for the project. Since this presentation was intended to promote the facility to the public, we tried to show the buildings in different settings to make the presentation more interesting and fun. We were lucky that the buildings were positioned near a lake and had connecting brides and activity. These items help create a nice illustration, as shown in figure 5.1.

Figure 5.1
One of the aerial views in the presentation.

Modeling

We modeled this project in 3D in Cadkey6 and imported the DXF file to the 3D Editor in 3D Studio. We started with a 2D plan and placed the plan in level one (or layer, if you are working in AutoCAD). All 3D objects were created in the remaining levels. Putting the objects in different levels enables you to easily maneuver the objects in Cadkey and then DXF several different files into 3D Studio Each object is color-coded in Cadkey with objects of the same material.

NOTE

Constructing your model in a CAD program offers advantages over constructing it in 3D Studio. You have more accuracy with your input. When you import everything into the editor from the CAD program, all 3D shapes are placed in exact locations—no fumbling around in the 3D Editor trying to get the shapes as close as possible. Using CAD programs to build in 3D does have some drawbacks, however; for example, your objects might come in with missing faces. To avoid missing faces, you need to simplify your shapes. Simplifying your shapes should be easy, since most architecture consists of simple geometric shapes.

The mesh for this project was extremely complex. We followed certain steps to ensure that we would not spend a lot of time organizing the objects in 3D Studio. If you plan and organize your mesh before importing the file, once in 3D Studio, you can immediate begin mapping and lighting the objects in your scene.

◆ All the buildings were modeled in Cadkey and the DXF imported to 3D Studio. Because the project was an animation that would show the entire project, all sides of the building were created in Cadkey. Figure 5.2 shows the completed mesh of the office building.

Figure 5.2

The completed mesh of the office building.

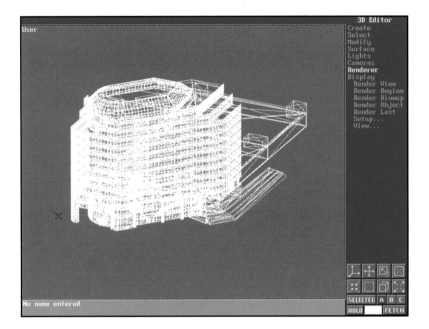

◆ We made sure the different sides of the building could be deleted if not needed in a particular rendering. This decreases the amount of faces, and in turn, decreases rendering time. The back of the buildings was not necessary for eye-level stills and was deleted in their files.

◆ For the night view, we added more detail in the lower interior space. More detail was needed because of all the lighting we would put inside. We used the same mesh for the interior image.

◆ Our sites are always a mesh. If you are doing animation, you might be able to use a mapped site; unfortunately, a mapped site almost always looks like a mapped site in a rendered image. You see much more detail in the higher-rendered images. Curbs, berms, and variations in landscape are all an important part of the site detailing.

- The mall in the background of the aerials was extruded from a plan and photographs to give heights.

- All the objects were imported to 3D Studio a few shapes at a time to maintain a certain level of organization and to make sure the objects entered 3D Studio correctly.

- Once in 3D Studio, we changed the name of the objects using the Attribute function, so the objects could be better identified. The color of the wireframe also was changed. All objects of the same material were given the same color wireframe. You can assign material to objects that require the same material simply by applying the material by color.

Organization is very important when creating objects and importing the DXF files into 3D Studio. If you are organized with your modeling and importing, you gain speed and finish this time-consuming part faster and easier. You will be able to put materials on the objects quicker and complete your projects in an adequate time frame.

Before importing any DXF files in 3D Studio, we created some basic materials in the 3D Materials Editor and named the materials the correct name for the object. When an object is imported in the 3D Editor, a material can also be assigned to the object at that time. You can go back to the Material Editor and change the material at any time. Assigning the material at the beginning assures that all objects will have the correct material. We selected the outside face of the glass and assigned another material, which makes it easy to make the building glass material an automatic reflection map. You might think all the planning we do importing files to 3D Studio is a bit excessive. When we import an object, we rename the object, color-code the wire-frame, and put a material on the object. If you have ever dealt with huge meshes with over 500,000 faces and hundreds of objects, you know how important organization is.

Whenever I do a still scene, I always model enough of the building that I can later create an animation. You never know if your client might come back and want an animation or more still images.

Mapping and Materials

We started placing the materials on the office building first. The office building was the main selling point at the time of the presentation. It was the building that the architects designed in the greatest detail and would be the first building constructed.

The office building consists of three different colors of green glass, broken down to vision glass and spandrel glass. The penthouse and some of the first-level glass are the medium color of green vision glass, whereas the main entry is composed of clear glass. All the glass, except for the clear glass, did not have any transparency. The mullions and columns are a gray metal. Phong shading was used for all the materials, and for all the objects in the renderings.

We started with the Diffuse color of the object first (the middle tones of your material), and then did the Ambient (the shade color) and Specular (the highlight color) colors. The Diffuse color was the exact color of the sample of the glass.

The Shininess and Shin. Strength settings in the Materials Editor were used to control the size and strength of the material's highlights. Shininess determines the size of the highlights, while Shin. Strength controls the intensity of the highlights. Because I did not create a difference in the two types of glass—vision and spandrel—using transparency, I increased the Shin. Strength on the vision glass so that it would appear lighter.

The mullions were a mid-gray tone material with 10% Shininess applied to them. I wanted them to have a matte finish with very little highlight. The columns were also a mid-gray color material with an 18% Shininess and 20% Shin. Strength applied to them. I wanted them to read like a metal object, but I did not want their intensity to be so overpowering that it took away from the glass.

The clear glass on the lower level is 80% transparent with a Diffuse color of dark gray and a Specular color of white. It has a Shininess and Shin. Strength of 20% and 28%, respectively.

Materials with solid colors and no mapping were created and placed on the objects in the interior of the lobby. The night image also had solid colors applied to the interior objects. While the night scene showed more mesh detail, your view was so far away from the building that the mapping would not show.

The material used for the roof of the office building was a darker gray color with a slight 5% texture map, and again the cement.cel was used. The roof needs to contrast with the sides of the building to help define the shape of the building in the illustration. Creating simple items, like parapets, also helps define the shape of the buildings.

For the dusk or day scene, only the spandrel and vision materials were changed. In the Materials Editor, a texture map of the sky at 34% was added to the previous settings of the spandrel glass. To make the glass appear brighter, the Shininess and Shin. Strength were intensified. The final material for the medium green spandrel is shown in figure 5.3.

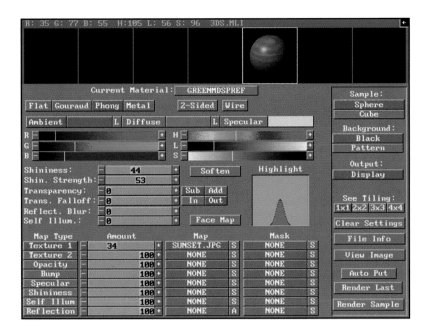

Figure 5.3

The material used to create the reflection effect in the glass, on the dusk image.

The materials for the clear glass at the entry and the bridge were the only changes made to the office building in the night rendering. The materials were made 100% transparent. The other buildings were simpler in detail design and did not have as many materials and as much detail. Both buildings were different colors of concrete. The hotel had a blue-green glass for the upper floors and a gray glass for the lower floors, whereas the condominium just used a gray glass.

We created three materials in the Materials Editor that were three shades of gray concrete. The Shininess and Shin Strength were set low at 8% and 10% so that the materials would appear to have a matte finish. The materials were then applied to different objects by like color in 3D Editor.

The glass in both buildings had less Shininess and Shin. Strength than the glass in the office building. We wanted the two buildings to be more subdued to bring out the office building.

The material used on the roof in the office building was also used on the hotel and condominium.

Materials were created for all objects in the scene. Different sky backgrounds were used in the dusk and night scene.

The bridge that connects the office building to the hotel had clear glass— the same glass material used for the office building. Two shades of concrete were created in the Materials Editor and applied to the columns that support the bridge. One was given a darker gray Diffuse color than the other concrete material. Both had 10% Shininess and 15% Shin. Strength added to the material.

The light bollards that are around the buildings were a matte gray material on the lower surface and a white glass with a slight transparency of 10%. The same white glass was also applied to the column lights on the bridge. For the night rendering, the white lights were changed to no transparency, and Self Illum. was increased to 80%.

We created the tennis courts and helicopter pad in Photoshop and mapped them onto a corresponding shape. Tan and gray cars were added to the scene, and boats were brought in and put in the water. Bright colors, such as red and yellow, were used for the boats.

TIP

Buildings usually are grays and tans. It is important to add spots of color in your illustration to enliven the drawing and generate interest. These spots of reds and blues could be cars, landscape, or people placed around the building. Placing plants and people near the entry of the building can add color and help draw your eye to the building. Any activity with which you surround the building only helps bring the scene to life.

For the grass, we used a flat dark-green color with a slight cement.cel bump map of 1%, and we placed 3D trees all around the site. The trees gave the grass enough texture, so no texture mapping was used on the grass. For the road, we used the cement.cel in your map directory as a texture map to give variation in the tone.

Because of the quick turnaround time this project demanded, we decided to go with a reflection map on the water and not use the water IPAS program. We wanted to keep consistency between the animation and the still images. The IPAS program for water would have taken too long to render in animation. To create the reflection in the water in the 3D Editor, we created an Lsphere that engulfed the project. We then flipped the Lsphere faces so the mapping would be on the inside faces of the sphere and put a sky reflection map on the object to create a moving sky reflection that occurs in the water throughout the entire animation. The face of the water object was selected. In the Materials Editor, a material with 100% flat reflection map and a Shininess and Shin. Strength of 60% and 67% was created and assigned to the selected face. The final material used for the water in the Material Editor is shown in figure 5.4.

The forest was created using the Silicon Garden IPAS program. We turned off the shadow casting and receiving in all the forest attributes box. This was to help decrease rendering time. For the still shots, we went into Photoshop and created some shadows for the trees.

Two of the illustrations needed background skies. I could not find a blue sky that complemented the green glass office building, so the day scene was changed to a more dramatic dusk scene. The sky in the night scene was a gradient background that went from near black to purple. The moon was created and placed in Photoshop and mirrored to create the reflection in the water.

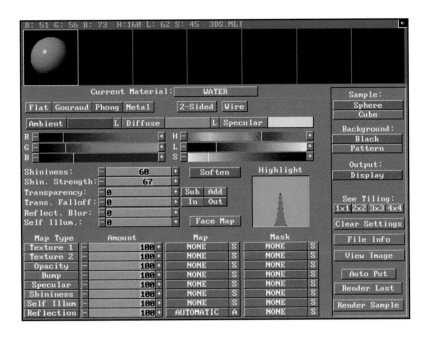

NOTE

Creating an early morning or evening shot can prove quite effective for creating a dramatic presentation. Before doing a day scene, show your client what you can do with the other times of the day. Photographers shooting outside shots will photograph objects in the early morning and late evening, because those times offer the best light of the day. Warm light and long shadows add mood and drama to your image.

Perspective

I cannot stress enough the importance of perspective. Perspective alone can determine the end result of your rendering, and using the computer makes achieving the best perspective of the building so easy.

Try to avoid the following mistakes when you create a perspective. Backing the camera too far can give your building a flat look and very little perspective (see fig. 5.5). On the other hand, getting too close to the building can lead to distortion and scale problems. The condominium is much taller than the office building in figure 5.6, but because of the closeness of the view, the office building looks much larger. The problem of distortion occurs frequently in interiors, as interiors are sometimes small rooms, and you are usually closer to objects in interiors. Try not to feel like you have to take the shot from inside the room. If you need to go into a hallway and take out the wall that obstructs the view, do so. If you do take the shot from inside the room, watch your viewing angle. If you see distortion of objects around the edges of your viewing angle, lessen your angle of view.

Figure 5.5

Moving too far back can reduce the perspective, making the buildings appear flat.

Figure 5.6

Moving too close to an object causes distortion and scaling problems.

Try to limit the use of three-point perspectives on ground levels and interiors. People view the world in three-point perspective, but they correct for skewed walls. You probably need to use a three-point on an aerial view. Try backing the camera away from the building and bringing in your FOV angle to compensate for the skewing of the vertical walls. Backing the camera up in an aerial view also puts all the buildings in a better relationship with one another, so

3D Studio Architectural Rendering

you don't end up with something like a five-story building in the foreground that looks twice as tall as a ten-story building in the background. Don't back up too much, though, or you lose your perspective.

On the aerial, we used a three-point perspective but backed the camera away from the buildings and brought in the FOV angle to reduce the effect of a three-point perspective and to make the scale of the buildings all the same. We set up the aerial perspectives in the keyframer and used one image as the beginning and the other as the end of the animation.

The perspective for the night scene also contributed to the animation. We used a two point perspective, taken about six feet above the office building first floor. We added bollards and lighting around the base of the building and along the river. Because 3D Studio offers no way to move your horizon without moving the view, we increased our FOV, rendered the image, and cropped for the final shot. A similar approach was used on the dusk scene, but the view was taken at a greater angle to get a dramatic shot of the building. We usually prefer more sky than foreground when we illustrate a building.

NOTE

Having done computer perspectives for more than seventeen years, I have concluded that an angle of between 30 to 40 degrees from the front of the building seems to work well. I also like to use a horizon height of around six feet. Try to keep the building as large in the view as you can.

Working with Lighting in 3D Studio

Once you have the mesh and mapping complete, you can start working on the lighting in 3D Studio. You need to decide on the time of day for the lighting. If you have chosen a background sky, you should have a good idea of the lighting setup. 3D Studio includes three different lighting sources with which the user can work: ambient, omni, and spotlight. Spotlights offer you the most control and are the only light capable of casting shadows.

Ambient Lighting

Ambient light works like an overall fill light. When you click on the Ambient light command, the Ambient Light Definition Box comes on the screen. This command only allows you to change the intensity and color of the overall light. Strong ambience reduces the all-important contrast in an image. You should keep an ambient light's intensity as low as possible. We moved all the sliders in the Ambient Light Box to 0, but ambient light can be useful for tinting your image a specific color.

Omni Lighting

Omni lights radiate evenly from a single source but cast no shadows. In the 3D Editor, choose Lights/Omni/Create and place the light source in one of your viewports rather than your Camera viewport to open the Omni Light Definition dialog box (see fig. 5.7).

Figure 5.7

The Omni Light Definition dialog box.

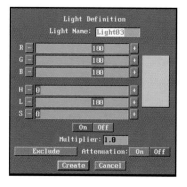

When the Omni Light Definition dialog box appears, you can change some of the settings or accept the defaults. Your omni light can be changed at any point in the rendering.

◆ The Omni Light Definition gives each light a Light Name as shown at the top of the box. You can rename the omni light any name.

◆ The upper sliders of the Omni Light Definition box enable you to change the color and intensity of the light.

◆ The on and off merely allow you to turn the light off and on in the scene. (Lights turned off will appear black in the scene.)

◆ The Multiplier enables you to increase or decrease the strength of the light. A higher number increases the strength while a lower number decreases the strength.

◆ The Exclude button enables you to exclude certain objects from a particular light.

◆ The Attenuation button enables you to turn the attenuation off or on. When Attenuation is set to on, you can restrict the lights path using ranges under the Omni Command in the 3D Editor. This is discussed under the Ranges in the 3D Editor.

◆ To create the light, accept the Create key; to cancel the command, hit the Cancel button.

Once you have created the light you have many options under the Lights/Omni commands to edit these lights.

- ◆ **Create.** Creates names and places an omni light in your scene. After you place the light, the Light Definition box appears. You use the slider tools at the top of the box to change the color of the light. You can use the On and Off buttons below the slider tool to make the lights active or inactive, respectively. The Multiplier edit box lets you increase or decrease the light's intensity. The Exclude button lets you exclude certain objects from the light source. Clicking on the Attenuate button to turn it on lets you determine the distance the for the light to fall.

- ◆ **Move.** Allows you to move your omni light.

- ◆ **Place Hilite.** Allows you to place a highlight on an object using an omni light. The command first asks you to place the highlight on the object in the rendering viewport. You then select the light you want to be responsible for the hiliting. The light moves to adjust for the highlight. Use omni lights created specifically to be used as highlights. You could get unpredictable results if you use omnis in the scene.

- ◆ **Adjust.** Allows you to adjust the omni after you have created the light. Select the omni light in the scene. The original light box comes up on the monitor and you can adjust the light at this time.

- ◆ **Ranges.** With attenuation button on, first hit the appropriate omni light in the scene. You will place two circles in the view. Place the first circle where you want the even intensity of the light to end and the second circle where you want the falloff of the light to end.

- ◆ **Delete.** Deletes your light source.

The next figures illustrate how the Range setting works with attenuation. figure 5.8 shows the setting for a normal omni light with attenuation off. The light encompasses the entire box. Figures 5.9 and 5.10 show the same omni light with attenuation on. Notice the two circles indicating ranges in figure 5.9. Only a specific area of the box has light hitting it as a result of using attenuation.

An alternative way to picking your light source from the viewport, is pressing the H key to bring up a light you can then adjust or delete.

Figure 5.8

A wall with attenuation off and the rendered results.

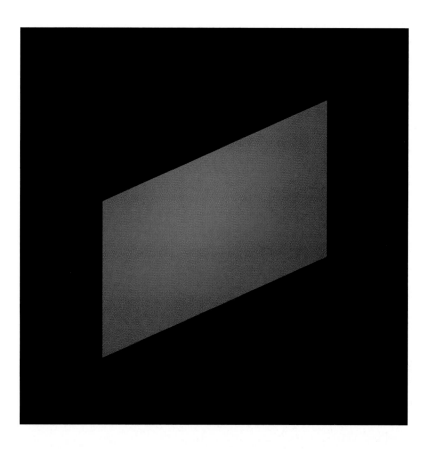

Figure 5.9

The exact light used to create figure 5.7, but with attenuation on. In the Top viewport, you see the two black circles.

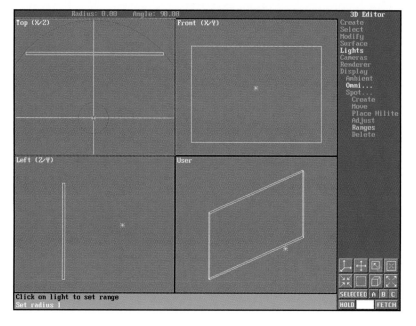

Figure 5.10
The rendered results with attenuation on.

Spotlights

Spotlights are the only lights in 3D Studio that can cast shadows. You can have as many spotlights in your scene as your scene needs. Spotlights with Shadows Casting turned on can greatly increases your rendering time depending on the amount of lights and the Shadow Map settings of these lights.

Note

Spotlights with a large shadow map do increase your rendering time significantly by consuming plenty of RAM. If you're serious about doing quality architectural renderings, you might need more RAM to allow you to use as many lights as necessary in a scene and render a scene in a few hours without swapping to your hard drive. When the computer has used up the RAM available and goes to the hard drive, rendering time dramatically increases.

3D Studio enables you to look down the path of your spotlight so that you can see specifically what objects are within the hotspot or falloff of the light. After you create the light, press Shift+$. The active viewport shows the spotlight and the area in which your light is aimed at the object. If you have many lights, a Spotlight Selector will appear on-screen so that you can pick the light you want to view. This enables you to know if the objects are all in the light source and what the hotspot and falloff are hitting. Figure 5.11 shows the Spotlight Definition dialog box.

Figure 5.11

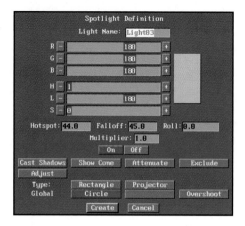

Select Lights\Spotlight from your 3D Editor. Place the light source and the target, and the Spotlight Definition dialog box appears.

◆ **Create.** Creates a spotlight by letting you first place the start position of the light and second place the direction of the light. At this point, the Spotlight Definition dialog box appears and you create and name the light. You can use the sliders to pick the color of your light like you did in the Omni Light Definition dialog box. The Spotlight Definition dialog box shows you the default Hotspot, Falloff, Roll, and Multiplier values. You can accept the default values and revise them later. Below these edit boxes are the Cast Shadows button and the key for adjusting the shadows. You can click on the Show Cone button to show the cone of your light, the falloff and hotspot. The Attenuation button works like the Attenuation button in the Omni Light Definition dialog box. The Spotlight command also lets you exclude certain objects from the light source. Figures 5.12 and 5.13 shows how the Exclude button works in the Omni Light and Spotlight commands.

Note in figures 5.12 and 5.13 that even after you exclude an object from a spotlight with shadows turned on, the object you excluded still has a shadow from that light source.

Tip

The Exclude button is very important in architectural illustration. You might want to limit some of the objects around the building from the main or fill light to make them darker. This effect of darkening objects around the perimeter of your drawing will draw your eye to the main subject matter, the building. Throw two spotlights into the scene at the same position, make the second light darker than the first, and exclude the surrounding building from darker spotlight. This highlights your building while slightly darkening the surrounding buildings. You can experiment with the exclude button using fill lights without shadow-casting capability.

Figure 5.12
The scene with no objects excluded.

Figure 5.13
The Exclude button can be useful when you want to exclude objects in the scene from a light source. The outer objects have been excluded from the light and appear dark.

At the bottom of the spotlight Definition dialog box, you can choose between the Rectangle or Circle buttons to select the shape of the your light. The Projector lets you project a bitmap or an animation through the light. You assign the bitmap by clicking on the Projector button and the button beneath it. The Overshoot button acts like an omni light and doesn't confine the light to the falloff, yet retains the cast shadows capability of a spotlight.

- **Moves.** Moves the spotlight. To make both ends of the light move, press the Ctrl key, and to copy the light, hold down the Shift key and move the newly created light. A Name for New Object box will appear, allowing you to name the new light.

- **Place Hilite.** Acts like the same command in Omni Light. You pick a specific area for your highlight in the rendering viewport and then pick the spotlight. The target and light both move to the location of you highlight.

- **Hotspot.** An area that defines the greatest intensity of your light. Must be smaller than your Falloff.

- **Falloff.** An area that defines from the strongest area of light to the fading of your light source.

- **Roll.** Rotates the spotlight around the axis using the center of the fallout point as the rotation axis. (You use Roll only when you work with a rectangular or projector light.)

- **Dolly.** Works like the camera dolly and moves the light toward or away from its target.

- **Adjust.** The original Spotlight Definition dialog box appears and lets you make any changes to your original light.

- **Aspect.** Changes the aspect ratio of a rectangular light source.

- **Bitmap Fit.** Used when using a rectangular projector light. This adjusts the aspect ratio of your rectangular light to fit the selected bitmap file.

- **Ranges.** This command works like Ranges option in the Omni Light. When you are prompted to create the two circles in a viewport, you must remember that you are not dealing with a flat circle of light, but a sphere. The light within the ranges will be in all coordinate systems.

- **Delete.** Deletes a spotlight.

TIP

For certain functions dealing with omni and spotlights, you can call up a list box from which you can select any of your omni and spotlights by pressing the h key. To copy a light, press the Shift key and select the light. To copy and move both the spotlight and its target, press Ctrl+Shift and move the light to its new position. You are not restricted to using the default names for your lights. You might rename the lights to a name that describes the function of the light in the scene.

Casting Shadows in 3D Studio

Casting shadows in 3D Studio is as easy as creating a spotlight, turning the Shadow button on in the Spotlight Definition dialog box, and rendering your scene. Shadows will appear on the screen in the direction of the light source. Choose Lights/Spotlight/Adjust to open the Spotlight Definition dialog box. Turn on the Shadow button and click on the Adjust button to see the current settings for the light's shadows. These are the Global Settings. Turn off the Global Settings and turn on the Shadow Maps button to change the settings. You can find all the controls for your shadow in the Local Shadow Control dialog box (see fig. 5.14).

Figure 5.14

The Local Shadow Control dialog box in 3D Studio.

◆ **Map bias.** The default setting is 1.0. Although 3D Studio recommends using 1.0 for architectural modeling, we usually use a smaller number. This setting connects the model to its shadow, and the lower the number, the better the connection—within limits. Unfortunately, using too low of a number can cause streaking at the outer edges of the shadow.

◆ **Map size.** Used only with shadow maps. The default setting is 512. We use a map size of between 1500 and 2000 for most of our illustrations, although using a higher map size increases your final rendering time. We find that 1500 for a map size gives the soft shadows we like in renderings. But the distance of your light source from the objects in the scene also affects the softness of your shadow.

◆ **Map sample range.** The default setting is 3. The sample range affects the edges of the shadow; the smaller the values, the sharper the edges. You can get some strange effects if you increase the value of the sample range past 5. We usually accept the default. Increasing the sample range will also increase your rendering time.

♦ **Ray Traced Shadows.** Turn on the Ray Trace button to render ray traced shadows. Furnishes the most accurate way to cast shadows in 3D Studio. Unfortunately, ray traced shadows will consume much rendering time.

♦ **Ray trace bias.** The default is 1.0. The Ray trace bias affects the distance between the object and its shadow; the smaller the number, the less the space.

♦ **Use Global Settings.** Uses the default settings. Turn the key off if you want to use Shadow Maps or Ray Traced Shadows.

Although ray traced shadows can offer you the most accurate shadows, they are far from being realistic-looking shadows. Their edges are way too sharp and dense and can distract strongly from a scene. Figure 5.15 shows the difference between the shadows cast using a shadow map versus using ray tracing.

Figure 5.15

You see the contrast between the sharp edges of ray traced shadows and the softer edges of shadow maps.

Shadow map

Figure 5.15
Continued

Ray tracing

The quality of your shadows are affected by many other elements in 3D Studio's lighting. The distance between your light source and your object affects the sharpness of your shadows: an increased distance will create softer shadows, and a decreased distance will make sharper edges on your shadow. The Hotspot and Falloff commands also affect the sharpness of the edges of shadows, and thus, their quality. Similar values for Falloff and Hotspot produce sharp-edged, unrealistic shadows, but a reduced Hotspot and increased Falloff produces softer, more realistic shadows. Figure 5.16 shows the difference between casting shadows using nearly identical Hotspot and Falloff and using a reduced Hotspot and increased Falloff.

Figure 5.16

The difference between having the hotspot and falloff close in size and reducing the hotspot and increasing the falloff.

The hotspot and falloff near the same size

Reduced hotspot, increased falloff

Lighting the Aerial View

We used simple lighting on the aerial, consistent with the lighting we used for the animation. We placed two spotlights on either side of the group of buildings. One spotlight generated the shadow and the other spotlight acted as a fill light and had less intensity.

When you place your light, do not place it at a 45 degree angle to the buildings. Move the light more to the side that you intend to receive the most light, to create better contrast between the sides of the building. See figures 5.17 and 5.18.

NOTE

Figure 5.17

Lighting set up properly to achieve contrasts between the planes of the box.

Figure 5.18

Lighting set up incorrectly, it does not achieve contrasts between the planes of the box.

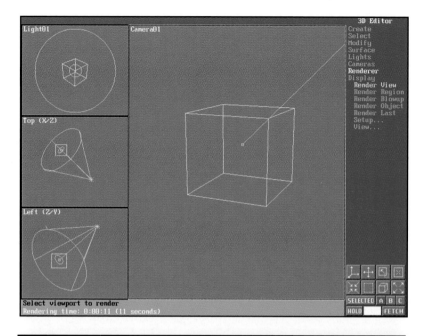

The color of the light was set to 180,180,180 for the one spot that generated the shadow. The color on the fill light was set to a darker, warmer color. A spotlight was used as a fill light instead of an omni light. The rendering time would be faster using an omni light, but the spotlight gives you much more control in the direction of the light. With the spotlight you can place the falloff and hotspot so that you get the effect of darkening edges around the image. Shadows are important on aerials, because they define the area of the building and help it sit on the site rather than appear to float. The Shadow Map was set to 1200 and the Map bias set to 1. Figure 5.19 shows the lighting setup for the aerial renderings.

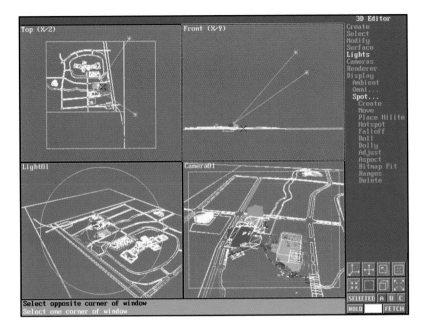

Figure 5.19
The lighting setup for the aerial view.

When you work with aerials and several buildings, you might need to light the buildings individually to get a consistent contrast between the buildings.

Lighting the Dusk Scene

We used a warmer spotlight (we increased the Shadow Map to 1500) for the main light that generated the shadow. We reduced the angle of the light to create longer shadows. The fill light was a slightly cooler light, with color setting of 30,29,32. Another spot was placed inside the building to highlight the interior. We turned on Shadow Casting in this interior light and reduced the Hotspot. We used a pale yellow in the interior light, and positioned the interior spot to hit one of the interior walls. The dusk scene's lighting final setup is shown in figure 5.20.

Figure 5.20

The dusk scene's lighting setup.

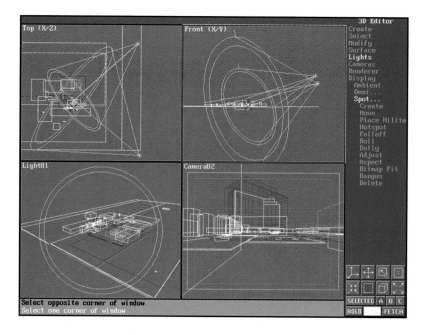

Lighting the Night Scene

Night scenes require a multitude of omni and spotlights to make the scene look real. When you see a building at night, you see lights everywhere. Lights occur in the interiors of the buildings and all around the base of the buildings. You have street lights and car lights, and some buildings even have lights on top of their roofs.

Even though it is a night scene, you still need a fill light to distinguish the shapes of the buildings. We positioned the fill light low to the ground and gave it a color of 19,21,24.

Night time gives all objects a tint of blue. Contrast still should exist between the different planes in a night scene, so we brought in another light and placed a stronger color of blue on it. You see the highlights on the left of the office building as a result of this light.

Every other bollard is a spotlight positioned above the bollard and target is directed towards a wall or the water. Your spotlight needs to be aimed at some object to show. Remember we made the bollards a white neon material ,so they would appear to glow. For the bollard lights, we turned off Shadow Casting and gave them a color of 230,173,84. We increased the Falloff to create more light hitting the walls. The two bollards at the front of the office building were directed at the main entry. We excluded all objects from this light except the entry and interior.

Two spots were placed in each light fixture on the bridge columns. One set of lights was created and copied to the other positions. The lights were pointed towards the column in an up-and-down direction. We excluded all objects from these lights except all the elements of the bridge. Again, we used a yellow-colored light with a large falloff.

Remember, if you do not turn on Shadow Casting, the spotlight acts like an omni and fails to stop at surfaces, generating unpredictable results. If you want a light to hit only a specific surface, you can exclude all other objects from that light.

STOP

The lights inside the bridge are a series of spotlights. The hotspot was reduced and the falloff was increased. Again the light was a yellow tint and every object was excluded from these lights except the bridge. The lights were positioned right under the ceiling of the bridge and the target was pointed at the outside mullions. One spotlight was created and copied to all the other locations. The interior of the building consisted of 10 spotlights all placed so the light would hit walls. Figure 5.21 shows the lighting setup for the office building and bridge. The exterior was excluded from these lights to keep it dark and the interior would stand out. One spotlight was used to blast the condominium with light. Again the shadow casting was turned off and the falloff was brought way out. All the objects except the condominium were excluded from this light.

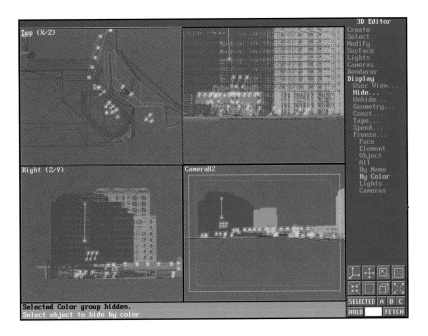

Figure 5.21
The final lighting used for the night scene.

The exclude option is useful when dealing with a complex mesh. You can light one object to your satisfaction and not have to worry about the light's effect on other objects in the scene. You just exclude the objects from the light source.

All together in this scene, we used 65 spotlights. You might not need this many spotlights to create a night scene, but we really wanted to make the building look lit up inside to create an appropriate mood for an evening scene.

Lighting Interior Spaces

Interior lighting can be trickier than any outside lighting. Your light sources come from all different directions. Different interior lights omit different colors and intensity of light. If you look at a room, you will notice that the walls aren't lit evenly. You can get some nice conical effects from certain lighting, as shown in figure 5.22. Lights from different sources create different shapes on the walls. Also, the ceiling, usually a light color because of the lack of light hitting it, appears much darker. If you have sunlight entering the room, you need to simulate that effect. If you just blast light into the room, you just get evenly lit walls that come off flat-looking. Avoid any kind of hard shadows, keep the shadows soft. Create enough lighting hitting the walls to make it interesting. Keep your hotspot reduced and enlarge your falloff to soften the edges of the cones of light hitting the walls.

Figure 5.22

The interior lighting for one of the images used for the presentation.

By authorization of WRT Energy Corporation

The Final Rendering

All five of the images were enlarged to 30×40 inches from a transparency. The finals were run in the 3D Studio renderer at 4000×3200 to fit into a 8×10 transparency. The rendering took anywhere from one hour for the night scene to eight hours for the aerials.

NOTE

Remember: Reproduction can take time. Depending on the final output, you can count on at least 24 hours per process. Enlargements of your final work will take several days because of the two processes involved: one day to make the transparency or negative and at least one day to make the print. Rush charges can cost as much as 200%. So, when you receive your deadline, keep in mind the reproduction time for developing the final image.

Summary

Lighting and shadows play an essential role in the way your eye sees architecture. Materials are defined by lighting, and shapes are determined by shadows. Lighting creates contrast between different planes of a building. Fine details of a building, such as joint lines, are exposed because of lighting and shadows. Lighting creates glass that is reflective during the day and transparent at night. The lighting controls in 3D Studio enable you to create these effects with surprising realism.

Lighting in 3D Studio can be compared to lighting in a photography studio. There are no formulas that work for everything. You need a basic plan or lighting concept to start with, but every image will need lighting adjustments to achieve the best results. The best images will be created by those who are willing to spend enough time and thought in this critical area.

Photographic Substitution

by Martha L. Rowlett
Houston, Texas

Author Bio

Martha L. Rowlett is a native Texan. She earned a bachelor's of science in environmental design from Texas A&M in 1978. Martha worked in architectural illustration and computer graphics for 17 years before starting her own firm in September 1995. Payne Rowlett specializes in architectural and engineering computer graphics.

Chapter Overview

The capability to place a 3D model into a photograph of an existing site is an effective method that architects and designers can use in client presentations. Placing the building on the proposed site enables the client to see a realistic representation of what the structure will look like on that site. With the capability of 3D modeling, illustrators no longer have to hand-paint a building onto a photograph but can digitally maneuver the image into the photograph. This process allows the illustrator to place the computer-generated image on the photograph and then manipulate the image to match the photograph's contrast and color. And now 3D Studio Release 4.0 has made the process of photographic substitution and perspective control easier with the addition of *camera control,* the manipulation the placement of an object to coincide with a background image. (Camera Control is discussed later, in the section "Setting Camera Angle and Perspective with Camera Control.")

Advantages

Instead of creating a model of a site, you may find that many projects are better suited for the photographic method. When the image requires specific landscaping or has existing buildings, a computer artist might choose to use a photograph. Creating a 3D landscape can be time-consuming task, for not only does the landscaping take up many faces in the mesh file, it also can greatly increase the final rendering time. Although 3D trees and plants might be sufficient for animation, still images require better and much more realistic plants than are now available in the 3D world.

Some illustrators, including myself, would rather use photographs of trees and plants, which can be masked or cloned into the final image. Although the quality of the planting is better using this method, the artist should be careful about matching the perspective and the lighting of the existing 3D image. Setting up the foreground and background of an aerial view can be extremely labor intensive, but by placing the building on a photograph, you decrease your modeling time, enabling you to focus on the main structure.

Disadvantages

Unfortunately, you may be limited by the quality of the photograph available of the site and the positioning of the 3D model on the photograph. Although costs may not always allow you to hire a professional photographer to shoot the photograph, taking out your instamatic and snapping a picture of the site would be far from adequate for most projects. Before deciding to use the photographic method, be sure that the main view of the building is not blocked by objects, such as trees and other buildings, that will prevent you from getting a photograph. Your goal should be to obtain the best perspective of your 3D model. Using an unsuitable photograph should never be an option;

instead, the computer artist should be willing to input the entire site. Remember the building is the main subject matter and should be the focus of your illustration. One advantage of computer illustration is the capability to create multiple views from one 3D model. Unless many photographs are taken of the site, placing the model on a photograph limits the illustrator to only one still view. The costs of scanning the photograph and outputting the image may also influence the final decision of whether to choose photographic substitution.

Photographic substitution is a useful tool for the 3D artist when used appropriately; it is the illustrator's job to determine if this method will obtain the best results for the client and the project.

The Project: Victoria House

Project Name: Victoria House

Location: Sydney, BC, Canada

Architects: Kevin Daly, Christopher Genik
                Santa Monica, CA

The model shown in figure 6.1 is a proposed house built on a sloping site in Canada. Because costs prohibited a trip to Canada and the existing structures around the resident were not a factor, another site was substituted. The photograph shown in figure 6.2 is actually a combination of several photographs combined in Photoshop.

Figure 6.1
The model of the proposed house.

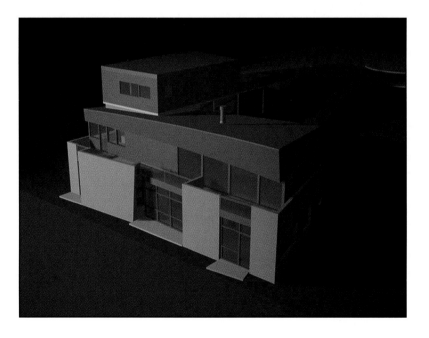

Figure 6.2
The photograph onto which the house was placed.

Scanning the Photographs

The next step, after determining that there is an available photograph, is to scan the photograph into the computer.

Before deciding on the type of scanning process, you need to determine what the final hard copy will be. Your service bureau should be able to determine what your dpi should be for the photograph by the final output. Getting the correct resolution is extremely important and will affect the quality of the final image. If the final image is to be an enlargement or film output, you will need to scan the photograph at a much higher resolution than if you were going to use 8×10 color copies.

Printing and scanning processes are constantly changing and being updated: call your service bureau and keep informed about the latest scans available on the market.

For this project, several slides were scanned onto a photo CD. The photo CDs can hold around 100 images from slides and stores these images at five different resolutions. The higher resolution 2048×3072 was the one imported for this project. This resolution has the capability to be printed out to 8×10 at a resolution of 300 dpi.

The following list shows other advantages of using a Kodak CD or Kodak Pro CD.

- The Kodak Pro CD has six resolutions available; the highest resolution can be used for poster-size images at 4096×6144. Because of the higher resolution, only about 20 images can be placed on a Kodak Pro CD.

- The Pro CD can also scan in 4×5 tranparencies as well as slides.

- The Kodak CDs are a great way to archive all your projects and images for future reference.

- You can access these files from Kodak's Access program or directly from Photoshop.

Because of the file sizes created when you have a slide or photograph scanned onto a CD, you will need some type of removable storage device. Your file sizes on a Kodak Pro CD can be as high as 72 MB. You will need a device to help you transport your file to and from the service bureau. Before purchasing a removable device, make sure your service bureau can support that drive and has the means to read a PC system.

Your service bureau may offer many choices for scanning your photograph: just make sure that they understand what the final output will be so that you will get the best results from the scan.

Modeling

In an animation, the viewer's eye is constantly moving, but when the model is stationary, the viewer has time to study the image. Animators sometimes reduce file size by eliminating minute details that are not apparent in animations. Because the viewer can study a stationary image longer, however, buildings should be modeled with much more detail than when modeled for an animation.

For this project, all 2D shapes were created in Cadkey 7. The meshes were saved to a DXF file for import into 3D Studio's Shaper. The shapes were extruded in the Lofter at the appropriate heights, and the objects were brought into the 3D Editor and then placed in the correct location. Because the final view had not been determined, the entire house was modeled front and back. The interior walls were created and furniture from existing models was introduced into the scene. The railings were a series of faces with a double-sided material assigned to them.

Because of the control you have in a CAD program, certain objects like the roof on this project might be easier to build in 3D in the CAD program and the 3D DXF file imported into the 3D Editor. The roof is a spline that slopes in two directions. CAD programs allow you exact input when building your models.

The key to creating a model is being organized. Don't try to DXF all the shapes at once. Combine all the similar objects and then color code the objects by material. Bring in shapes in a logical manner so you can make sure that every object has been modeled and there are no holes in the model. One advantage to architectural modeling is that the shapes are fairly simple geometric forms and can be easily constructed. You can buy programs that work with your existing CAD programs that automatically construct architectural objects in 3D.

Another problem illustrators have when DXFing 3D objects is missing faces. Keeping your 3D shapes simple helps to eliminate this problem. Also remember, your 3D objects have to be a solid model. If you cannot build your model in the real world, chances are the object will not go through 3D Studio correctly.

After the mesh was completed (see fig. 6.3), we started working on the mapping.

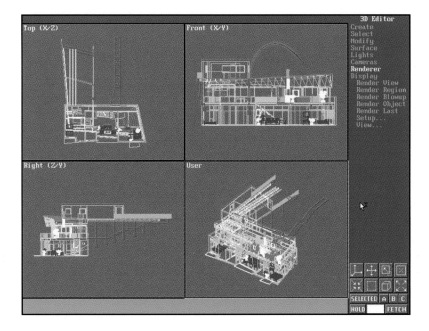

Figure 6.3
The completed mesh.

Mapping

The house is comprised of board-formed concrete at the base and cedar siding at the top. The handrails, frames, and roof are various kinds of metal. Because I could not locate the texture maps I needed on any existing files, I created the texture maps in Photoshop using a combination of noise, blur, and color balance and created evenly spaced lines to indicate the joints. Both materials were given a slight bump map in the Materials Editor. Figures 6.4 and 6.5 show the material setup for the concrete and cedar siding. The metals were all grey phong materials with certain degrees of shininess and shininess strength.

Figure 6.4
Material setup for concrete block.

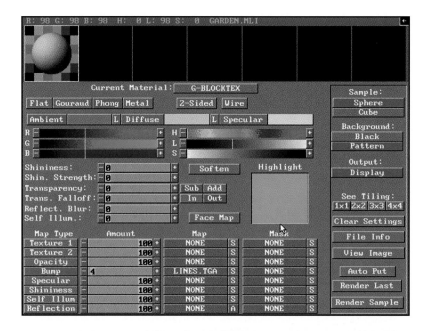

Figure 6.5
Material setup for the cedar siding.

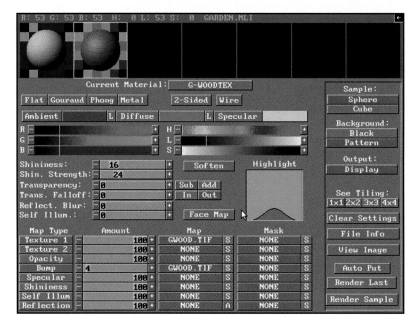

TIP

Remember that all objects should be color-coded or given like names in the 3D Editor, so that you can apply a material to all like objects with one keystroke or use the first letters of the name in the name object box.

The glass in architecture can be the most important element. Glass helps draw the viewer's eye to the middle of the picture. We created the glass with a gray 100% transparent material with 50% shininess and 70% shininess strength. The cast shadows, in the Object Attributes, was turned off for all the glass. This allows light from the inside of the house to pass through the glass and shine on the outside walls.

This project consists of objects that are neutral grays. Color was added to objects inside the house to help add life to interior and bright colors to the illustration.

Materials can take on a different quality when rendering at high resolutions. The material may appear fine on your low resolution monitor, but once you have rendered the image in high resolution, the bump maps may appear much more pronounced. You might want to reduce the amount of bump map when rendering at high resolution. Again, organization can be important when applying materials and mapping the scale of the maps onto the objects. I always use the Mapping command under the Surface command in 3D Editor. The maps are easier to scale to their exact proportions using this Mapping command. Here is the procedure for mapping on a scale of a texture map:

1. First select one face of the object. If the model is relatively simple, you can select all the faces of that object that are facing one direction. Choose Create/Face/Detach and rename those faces as another object.

2. Do this same procedure on all sides of the object that will need to have separate mapping coordinates.

3. Choose Surface/Mapping/Adjust/Bitmap Fit and find the map you created. The rectangle will now take the form of your map.

4. After you create your maps or if you are using an existing map, go into the Image Browser or press the F6 key and determine the height of the map. (If your map is five bricks high, then you know the map should be about 20 inches high.)

5. View align the rectangle with the appropriate viewport. Remember the map is situated correctly if the green line is always on the right of the view with which you are aligning the map.

6. Apply the mapping coordinates to the face by choosing Surface/Mapping/Apply to Object. After you apply the mapping to an object, keep the horizontal plane of the mapping coordinate the same. This will ensure that all your horizontal brick or wood joints will line up at the corners of your objects.

Now you have created maps that are exactly proportional to the object and material, and your materials will appear more realistic. You are now ready to view your model in 3D Studio.

Setting Camera Angle and Perspective with Camera Control

Setting up the right perspective is important in any architectural illustration. The Camera Control in 3D Studio provides you with ultimate control for setting up your perspective. 3D Studio has made the task of setting up your view easier, but the user must remember the basics of perspective in order to create the best view of your building. The world is composed of three kinds of perspective: one-point, two-point, and three-point. All of these perspectives have lines that converge at the horizon line. The horizon line represents the viewer's eye location in relationship to the ground plane. The lines of the model that converge at the horizon line represent the vanishing lines in the view. The point at which the lines meet the horizon is called a *vanishing point*.

♦ **One-point perspective.** In a one-point perspective, all the horizontal lines of a model converge at the horizon line at the same point on that line. A one-point perspective has one vanishing point. The location of the camera and target should be the same distance from the ground plane. One-point perspectives are usually used when dealing with interior spaces such as long hallways.

♦ **Two-point perspective.** Most illustrators choose to work in the two-point perspective. The horizontal lines converge at two different places on the horizon line to form a two-point perspective. There are two vanishing points in a two point perspective. To achieve a two-point perspective in 3D Studio, the camera and target positions have to be the same height (usually illustrators choose a viewing height of five to six feet).

♦ **Three-point perspective.** When the camera and the target are at different heights, you have created a three-point perspective. Buildings seem to look better in two-point perspective; you do not have the angled walls that you get with three-point perspective. The human eye is constantly viewing the world in a three-point perspective, but will correct the vertical aspect of walls. Using three-point perspective for aerials and interior atrium views seems to work well.

3D Studio does not allow the viewer to move the horizon up and down in the viewport without moving the camera. This can be a problem in architectural renderings, because illustrators generally like to show more sky and less foreground. If it becomes necessary to use a three-point perspective, you can minimize the convergence of the third vanishing point by backing the camera away from the object and bringing in your field of view (FOV), which is the same as using a longer lens. This compensates for the third vanishing point and makes the walls appear more vertical.

Even when you select a photograph that represents the best angle for the building, you probably will have to adjust the angle of your building to fit the photograph. 3D Studio provides you with the Camera Control feature to help place your model perfectly into a photograph.

Before beginning camera contol, you need to make a low-resolution image of your background photograph. Make sure that the proportions of the low resolution remain the same as the higher resolution photograph by changing only the pixel size of the image. This will speed up the resizing process in the camera control and optimize the amount of RAM being used. You must have one light on the scene for the image to appear; otherwise, everything will appear black. If the entire model does not have to be used to determine the camera angle, select the objects you wish to use before entering Camera Control.

1. Make sure that the Camera viewport is active and select Camera/Prevu or press the F7 key. Now you are in Camera Control, and you see your image generated in Phong shading with a black background.

2. Bring in the low-resolution background by selecting Background, and then select Bitmap to bring in your background image. Camera Control automatically resizes your photograph to fit. In the camera view, you will see your image and the background photograph.

3. Click on the Horizon button to see the horizon line (see fig. 6.6). This is the horizon line as it relates to your image. If you need to change the color of the horizon line to make it more visible, click on the C button next to the Horizon button. When the color option appears, revise the color and select OK.

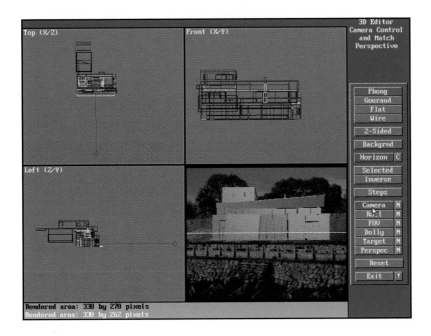

Figure 6.6

The image in Phong with background and horizon line.

A *horizon line* is the line that represents the viewer's eye horizontal to the ground. All horizontal lines of the photograph and building, in perspective, will converge at the horizon line. The points where these lines converge on the horizon are called *vanishing points*. Locating the horizon helps you find the vanishing points of the image and photograph and aids you in matching the perspectives.

Setting View and Movement Options

Before you complete the setting of camera angle and perspective, you may want to establish the most practical view and mouse movement for the project. Camera Control enables you to set view and mouse movement control to your liking with several of its commands.

Viewing Options

The Camera Control allows you to render your image using different rendering qualities. Camera Control, like the Preview command, does not show mapping. Wire mode is the fastest way to view your model. Click on the Camera Control's Wire button to see your building in a mesh form (see fig. 6.7).

Figure 6.7

The building in wire form.

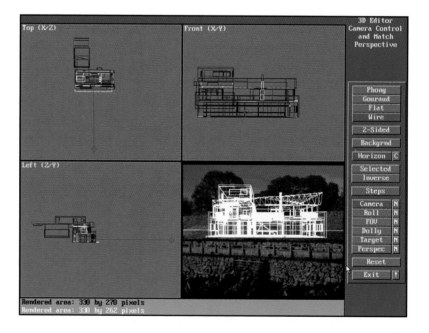

Other viewing options available in Camera Control are as follows:

♦ **Phong.** Shows highlights and gives the best display.

♦ **Gouraud.** Displays smooth shading.

♦ **Flat.** The fastest solid modeling display.

You might want to use the fastest renderer available in camera control, the wire. If you are dealing with a complex model, you might want to choose one of the other methods of display. Because your wireframe is complex, you will have too many lines on your screen and might not be able to see where your vanishing lines are. Most systems can handle Phong mode without any problems.

To decrease your rendering time in Camera Control, it is best to to hide any objects that are not necessary to determine the perspective of the building. You can hide objects in the 3D Editor, but you also can hide objects within Camera Control. To hide objects in Camera Control, use the Select command in the 3D Editor and select the objects that will not be necessary in Camera Control. Go into Camera Control. Click on the Selected button and only the objects you have selected will be displayed. Click on the Inverse button and the correct objects will be displayed in the viewport. You want the Camera Control process to be fast. Minimize the mesh enough to able to determine the vanishing points and placement of the object within the photograph. A smaller mesh will speed up your time spent in Camera Control. Remember, you are not rendering the final image in Camera Control, but finding the location of the building in the photograph so you can run the final image.

Another command in the Camera Control is the 2-Sided button. I would leave the 2-Sided button off to speed up rendering time. This option helps display objects created in CAD programs that might have problems with inverted normals.

Mouse Movement

To obtain an accurate movement with your mouse, click on the Steps button to display the Keyboard Step Rate dialog box (see fig. 6.8), and change the distance to 1. (Holding down the Shift key while using the mouse will make the Step command a distance of .1.) Choose OK to accept this change.

Figure 6.8
The Keyboard Step Rate dialog box.

Locating the Horizon Line in Camera Control

The first step to positioning the building on the photograph is to locate the horizon line on your photograph. On my image, the horizon seems to be positioned right above the stone wall. The image will be in a slight three-point perspective, so the Target and the Camera will not be at the same vertical level. We will be dealing with the Target and Camera buttons in the Camera Control to place the horizon.

1. While in Camera Control, select the Target button and then click in the Camera viewport, or you can press the space bar.

2. Press the Tab key until the arrow on your screen is vertical. Then move your mouse up or down until the horizon line of your building matches the horizon line of the photograph.

3. Your Target might be in the right position, but your Camera will not be (unless you are dealing with a two-point perspective, in which both the Target and Camera would be at the same location). The viewing angle of this perspective is sightly lower than the target, so the Camera will be moved below the Target. Choose the Camera button and then the Camera viewport, keeping the arrows in the vertical position and, moving in an up and down position, adjust the horizon into the correct position. You might have to repeat steps 2 and 3 until you are satisfied with the placement of the horizon line. Figure 6.9 shows the final placement of the horizon line.

Figure 6.9

Place of final horizon.

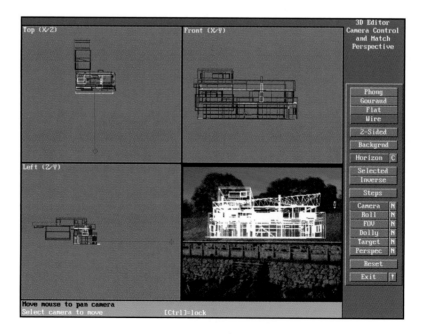

3D Studio Architectural Rendering

4. After locating the horizon, select the Camera button and then select the Camera view or press C. (You must always select the Camera view after clicking on one of the functions in Camera Control, or you can press the space bar.)

5. Press the Tab key until you see the arrow going horizontally. Move the building's perspective until the building lines up with the vanishing points. If the building has other structures that are vanishing to the same point, align your building with their faces. Figure 6.10 shows the perspective being adjusted in Camera Control.

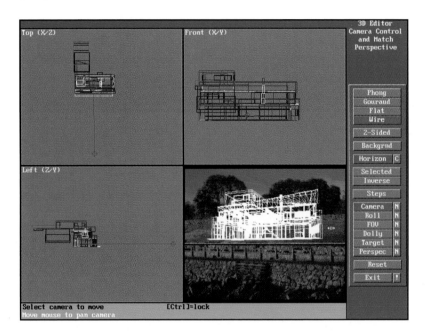

Figure 6.10
Moving the camera to the side to establish correct perspective.

Try to get the horizon and perspective as close as possible. Do one operation at a time until you have the results you want, before proceeding to the next. You will not be going from one command to another losing track of the last step you did and will be more organized about your approach in Camera Control. Again, you are dealing with a slight three-point perspective for this project. If you were working with a two-point perspective, after the horizon was established, all your camera functions would be moving only in the horizontal direction.

Setting the Scale

Next, we need to deal with the scale of the building in relation to its surroundings. For this project, we need to change the field of view and change the distance between the viewer and the structure. The FOV (field of view) option changes your viewing angle, and the Dolly option adjusts the distance from the camera to the target. The Dolly and the FOV functions in Camera Control work the same way as the functions of the same name in the Camera command in the 3D Editor. The Perspec option changes both the FOV and the Dolly. The FOV seems to be correct for this project, but the size of the building needs to be reduced. You need to select the Dolly option.

1. Choose the Dolly button and click in the Camera viewport or press the space bar.

2. Maneuver the image until it appears the right size.

3. Render the image with Phong shading and see if the results are satisfactory. See figure 6.11 for the final results of Camera Control.

Figure 6.11

Final camera control rendering.

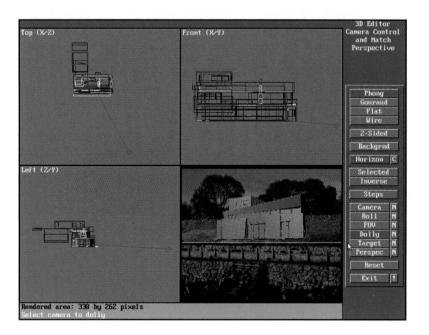

After obtaining the right view, click on the Exit button and accept the new camera angle. If you want to return to the original settings before selecting Exit, press Ctrl+A; or after clicking on Exit, click on No or Cancel to stay in Camera Control.

If you find the mouse difficult to control, 3D Studio camera control offers you another method to change the camera angle numerically. Click on the N button next to Camera to display the Camera Position dialog box (see fig. 6.12), which displays absolute and relative camera locations. This gives you the option to change the camera relative to the last position or to change to absolute (from the zero position).

Figure 6.12
Camera numerical input.

The following list shows the command in the Camera Control and the numerical input expected.

- The Target numerical input is similar to the Camera's input. When you hit the N button next to the Target button, you see two sets of numbers. One is the absolute position of the target, and the other set the relative position. The relative position will always be a set of zeros. You can change the position of your target by changing the absolute coordinates to your zero point or by relative coordinates to the current position indicated be your current absolute settings.

- The Roll numerical input gives you the current roll of the camera in degrees and the relative roll. This command allows you to roll the camera to a vertical view or a slightly angled view.

- The Dolly numerical input gives you the current distance to the target and the distance you will move from or to the target.

- The FOV input gives you the option of inputing a new field of view and or a new lens focal length.

- The Perspec option enables you to set the FOV and the Dolly distance numerically.

Numerical input gives you a much more accurate way to achieve a good match between the photograph and your model.

Lighting

After the view is established, you need to set up the lighting so that it matches the lighting of the photograph. This photograph (refer back to figure 6.2) was taken in the early morning, and therefore, you should construct your lighting appropriately. To create some interest in the building, light up the interior spaces.

Placement of lights in the illustration is important. Good contrast is important in architectural rendering. Lighting determines how much contrast the different planes of the building will receive. Here are some important things to remember in relation to this project about lighting, contrast, and interior lighting.

♦ Vary the amount of light that hits the walls to give a more realistic look to your interior.

♦ Turn on Shadow Casting in your Spotlight Definition Box. Spotlights without shadow casting on will act like omni lights, and the light will go through objects. With Shadow Casting on, the light will stop at the objects the light hits. You will have much more control over where your light falls and what objects your light is hitting.

♦ Direct the lights that are hitting the walls from the ceiling down towards the wall. The light will create some nice cone effects on the wall.

♦ The colors of the interior lights ranged from strong yellows to oranges. The interior spaces should look like they are glowing from the outside. Figure 6.13 shows the settings for a typical spotlight used in the interior.

Figure 6.13

The settings for a typical interior spotlight in the Spotlight Definition dialog box.

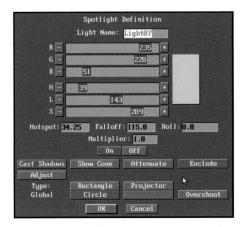

♦ The falloff was increased depending on the size of the wall it was hitting while the hotspot was reduced create a softer light.

♦ There were spotlights directed from the interior through the glass to cast shadows and light on the exterior wall. To enable spotlights to cast shadows through the glass, the Glass Shadow Receiving button in the Attribute Box was turned off.

♦ Two spotlights were placed as exterior lights on either side of the building. Because the scene was an early morning view, the exterior lights should be a warm light with a lower than normal intensity. The position of the lights and their targets should a little higher than the horizon line. One of the spotlights was used as a fill light. While many 3D Studio users use an omni as a fill light, I prefer using a spotlight. You have more control over the position for the light and where the light will fall in the scene.

◆ Omnis were placed in the scene to light the ceilings. The omnis were given a warm color and their intensity was decreased. All other objects were excluded from these lights. The Attenuation button in the Omni Definition Box was turned on and the ranges were adjusted to light certain portions of the ceiling. You are giving the ceiling a little variation of color by using ranges. If the ceilings were all one tone, they would look flat and unrealistic. Ceilings are generally white, but because lighting is usually pointed away from the ceilings, they usually appear darker. Keeping the ceilings dark will help with the contrast between the ceilings and walls and will make the image more realistic.

◆ This scene has a total of 29 spotlights and five omnis. Figures 6.14 and 6.15 show placement of all the lights in the scene from an elevation and floor plan.

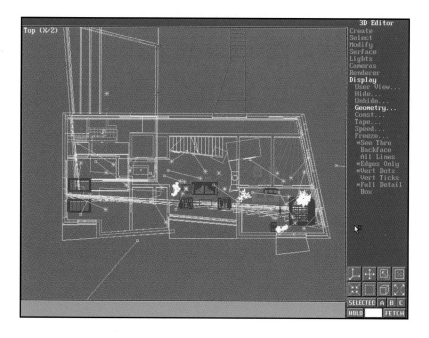

Figure 6.14
Placement of lights in the scene floor plan.

Spotlights, with the shadow on, increase the final rendering time. If the spotlights did not have the Shadow option on, the lights would not stop at the walls but would enter the next room. The spotlights would act like omni lights. You must turn on the shadow control to get the nice cone effects that you see in the interior. Just putting two exterior lights in this scene would not create the effect needed to give you a realistic image of the house.

Figure 6.15
Placement of lights in the scene elevation.

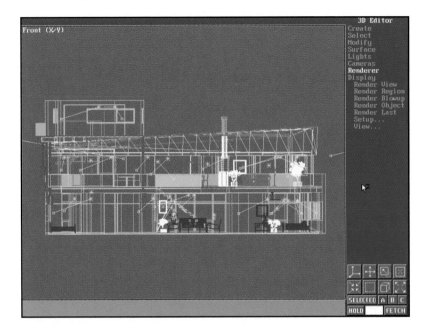

Combining the Images

You can combine the scene several different ways. After you are finished with the model, you can simply render the scene with the bitmap as a background in the correct resolution by using the 3D Renderer command. Or you can go into Video Post and combine and render the images. I prefer to combine the two scenes, in a photoediting program, because of the advantages of such programs. Any photographs of objects can be easily combined and edited for color and size. The contrast of the entire image can be changed instantly on your scene. There are endless possiblities in a program like Photoshop in combination with 3D Studio.

When the images are placed in a photograph and rendered in 3D Studio, objects might obstruct part of the building, or there may be problems with how the building sits on the site. Even if you render the house using the photograph background in 3D Studio, you will still have to edit the final image in the photoediting program. By combining the images in a photoediting program you can work with the contrast and color and can place and adjust the building on the site easier. It is like fine-tuning your image.

For this project, I used Photoshop 3.04 for Windows:

1. Bring the photograph and your final image rendered in 3D Studio into Photoshop.

2. Make the background color of your image created in 3D Studio a solid color not used in the scene, so that you can easily select the building.

3. First select the background color and then inverse the selection to select the building.

4. Copy and place the image into the photograph at the correct location.

5. At this point, you might have to adjust the contrast or colors of your image to match the photograph.

6. Save the selection of the building. Save the combined image and photograph under a different file name.

7. If the building cuts off objects that should be in front of the building, just go back to the original photograph, select those objects, and copy them in front of the building.

8. If the grass around the building needs to be worked on, mask off that area and rubber stamp the existing grass into those areas.

9. You can bring in other trees and people from other photos, but make sure that you keep them selected until you have matched the contrast and color of the photograph and the trees or people match the perspective of the photograph.

When the image is completed, you are ready to get the final output.

Rendering Your Image

When the model is finished and the lighting and camera angle are completed, you are ready to render your final image. You have determined what your final resolution should be by the final output. To render your image at a higher resolution, you will need to follow these steps. Be sure that your safe frame is on at the camera frame so that you can see how much of the image you are rendering.

1. From your 3D Editor, choose the Renderer command then the Render View command and select the viewport you want to render. The Render Still Image Box will appear on the screen.

2. Select the Configure option in the Render Still Image box.

Your computer can only display a resolution as high as your render display is configured for. So you can set the display driver to Null (or in the Render box select No Display.) Select OK to accept. Select the type file format you want to create from the top of the menu. For this exercise, I selected TARGA file. Enter the appropriate resolution in the Width and Height boxes, and enter the aspect ratio of one. For this image, the resolution was set at 2596×2066. Choose OK when your selections are finished.

Figure 6.16

Setting up the Device Configuration dialog box.

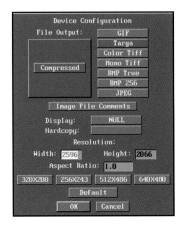

3. Select the Options button from your Render Still Image Box and increase your pixel size to 1.5. Choose OK to return to the rendering image.

4. From your Render Image Box, turn on your disk option, name the file, and render the image. Rendering high resolution images can take many hours. If you want to render large files, make sure that you have adequate RAM and disk space.

Output Options

Getting a hard copy replication of the image you see on your computer screen is not as easy as you might think. All monitors are calibrated differently, and results from printing processes differ. A recent illustration I completed went to four different processes, ending up with four totally different results.

Printing processes can be extremely exasperating. Finding a service bureau willing to work with you during the printing processes is important. If you are willing to stay with one bureau, consider calibrating your monitor to be compatible with theirs.

At the present time, printing computer images is not an exact science. Table 6.1 shows printing options now available with the recommended dpi and final size of the print. You should follow the recommended dpi and not exceed this amount. You would just be wasting computer run time. Find out what your service bureau offers and always keep abreast of what new printing techniques are becoming available.

Table 6.1   Printing Options

Type	Resolution	Image Size	Comments
Fuji Pictography (Fuji-Print)	Up to 400 dpi	Up to 8 1/2×11	This is the best direct printing method I have found. The images are sharp; the colors are accurate; and the turn-around time is fast. The process is limited by its size and costs.
Color copies (laser printers)	Depends on the copier	Up to 11×17	This process is good for quick presentations and proofing your final image. Watch for streaking and color changes.
Dye sublimation	Up to 320 dpi	Up to 11×17	Can be printed in either RGB or CMYK depending on your service bureau. You will encounter color shifts and streaking with this process.
Iris prints	Up to 300 dpi	Up to 30×40	Can be printed on different papers, and the final image is good. The dreaded RGB to CMYK conversion. Look for your image to change in contrast and have color shifts. Find a service bureau willing to work with you, and bring along color copy of what your image should look like.
Inkjet printing	Up to 300 dpi	Up to 52 inches	The final image may appear grainy. The colors are vivid, and this is one method that will allow you to get an enlargement of your final image. Make sure that you run the image at 300 dpi. The quality of the image goes down if the dpi is too low.

continues

Table 6.1 Continued			
Type	Resolution	Image Size	Comments
Film (slides, negatives, transparencies)			Consult your service bureau for the resolution you need and the final size you need to make your image. There are many different levels of quality and price. If your final product is to be a large print, I would suggest scanning your file to a color negative, and then have a standard photographic print made from the negative. If you are going to an 8×10 transparency, count on the final image size being large.

Summary

To be a computer illustrator, knowing the program is only one aspect you must learn. The processes of photography, scanning, and output methods are all subjects that the illustrator should know and keep up with in the ever-changing world.

Acquiring and learning a program like Photoshop should also be a priority in order to do quality editing. Computers are changing the way we view our world, and with the combination of photography and modeling, we can obtain a realistic image and increasingly better results.

Landscaping

by Todd Peterson
Knoxville, Tennessee

Author Bio

Todd is the owner of MTP Graphics, an architectural rendering, animation, multimedia, and training company located in Knoxville, TN. When he is not rendering and animating to his heart's content, he spends time teaching AutoCAD and 3D Studio at Pellissippi State Community College. In the past, Todd has also taught at the University of Tennessee College of Architecture. Additionally, Todd has authored other titles for New Riders Publishing, including *3D Studio for Beginners*, *Windows NT for Graphics Professionals*, and the *AutoCAD Performance Tuning Toolkit*.

Chapter Overview

Landscaping is the design of the site surrounding a building—one of the more difficult aspects of good architectural rendering. The better the landscape, the more realistic the building appears and the better rendering you can produce.

This chapter focuses on the aspects related to creating a landscape for a building. In particular, this chapter focuses on the following topics:

◆ The elements of landscaping

◆ Creating a site

◆ Atmospheric effects

◆ Tips and techniques

Elements of Landscaping

Before you can landscape an architectural building, you must create several distinct elements, including the following:

◆ The site

◆ Vegetation

◆ Road work

◆ Man-made items

Site

The *site* is the actual ground around the building. Sites generally are somewhat difficult to model, unless they're perfectly flat. Otherwise, you must deal with surfaces that constantly change slope and pitch.

The easiest way to create a site is to have someone else do it. If the project you work on is going to actually be built, someone somewhere undoubtedly has surveyed that site and entered the survey data into a CAD system. Most CAD systems can generate a 3D model of the site based on this information. If possible, try to get this 3D mesh in DXF form from the surveying company. If you can, then all you have to do is some simple modifications to match any changes you might need.

If you can't get a 3D site mesh from the surveyor, you can go about creating a site in one of several ways. One way is to draw the contours of the site and place the contours at their correct elevations and then create surfaces between those contours. You can create surfaces between contours most easily by using AutoCAD's RULESURF command and then importing the resulting mesh into 3D Studio. Another way is simply to plot survey points around the site. Fortunately, when it comes to architectural rendering, all you really need to do is approximate the site. No one knows the difference if you're off by a foot or two here or there.

As an alternative, several IPAS routines made specifically for creating sites also are available. Some of these IPAS routines use COGO (Coordinate Geometry) techniques to import survey data and generate a 3D mesh. In this case, you need to get the survey information from the surveyor, then you can enter the coordinates and generate the site yourself.

Vegetation

Vegetation is critical to a good-looking landscape. Unfortunately, the organic nature of vegetation can make creating it by hand extremely difficult. Several solutions are available.

First, you can purchase IPAS routines that generate the vegetation based on mathematical and fractal formulas. Two such routines are Yost Group's Silicon Garden and 4Dvision's Nursery module. Both create trees. Silicon Garden also helps you create other types of vegetation, such as flowers and plants. Unfortunately, creating highly detailed plants using these routines can prove rather expensive in terms of face count and file size. For example, the Nursery module easily can generate a single tree 10 MB in size.

NOTE

For more information on Silicon Garden, Nursery, and other IPAS routines, see New Riders Publishing's *3D Studio IPAS Plug-In Reference*.

If you can't afford these IPAS routines, you can create the geometry yourself or fudge it. One way you can fudge vegetation is to use a photograph. You can create a material based on the photograph, using diffuse and opacity mapping in the material. You can then map the material onto a single face or a two-sided crossing face to give the illusion of more depth. You end up with a flat tree, but oriented correctly, the viewer never notices. The section "Tips and Techniques," later in this chapter, discusses technique in further detail.

Backgrounds

For many projects, you often have access to the actual site with which you work. In this case, you can easily take a photograph of the site and use it as a background in your rendering to add an immediately noticeable, high degree of realism to your rendering. 3D Studio Release 4 supports perspective matching, to make your life easier.

Even if you don't have or want to use a photograph of the site, you still might want to use some sort of background, such as a photograph of clouds. Clouds are difficult to model and make look good. The best solution is to use a background of a photograph of real clouds. Your clients aren't likely to ever tell the difference.

The only shortcoming of using a background of clouds comes when you generate an animation of the building and site. As the camera travels around the site, the background always stays the same. Unfortunately, in real life, the background always adjusts to the new view. In 3D Studio, you can get around this by mapping the clouds bitmap to the inside of a sphere; then the clouds are static when you move through the animation—the way it should be.

Road Work

Many sites that you might have the opportunity to work on will involve some sort of road work. Road work can be a road, a sidewalk, or even a dirt path. You must always model this feature. The hard part is that it must match the surface of the site.

An incorrectly modeled road might exhibit all sorts of funny features when rendering. The road might float above the ground, for example, or it might appear to be partially buried in the site. The best solution is to obtain the site mesh after the surveyor has added a road to it. Otherwise, you need to do some work in the 3D editor to get clean-looking road work.

Man-Made Items

The last items generally considered part of a landscape are man-made items. Man-made items include, but aren't limited to, lights, fences, cars, people, benches, fountains, and so on—just about anything man can make and place on a site, other than the main building.

Lights, of course, are very important for the overall mood and appearance an exterior scene. You can create streetlights, house lights, ground lighting, and so forth. The only thing you really need to remember when you create exterior lights is that many exterior lights use a different type of lamp, which translates to slightly different colors of light on the exterior. A sodium light has a distinct orange glow, for example, whereas a regular streetlight might have a rather sterile white-blue-purple look.

When you work with man-made items, you should try to populate your site accordingly. If you place cars and people on the site, you want to be sure not to place too many or too few people for the context of the site. A park might have many people and cars in and around the site, for example, whereas the site for a house might have only one or two cars and/or people.

So, several elements are necessary to create effective landscaping. Combining these elements in a thoughtful and concise manner can produce landscaping that adds to, rather than detracts from, the architectural rendering you produce.

The Gazebo Project

In the next couple sections, you generate and populate a landscape for a gazebo and accompanying fountain. Figure 7.1 shows you the gazebo and benches you use to begin. Figure 7.2 shows you the resulting landscaping and lighting at the end of the exercises.

Figure 7.1

The gazebo beforehand.

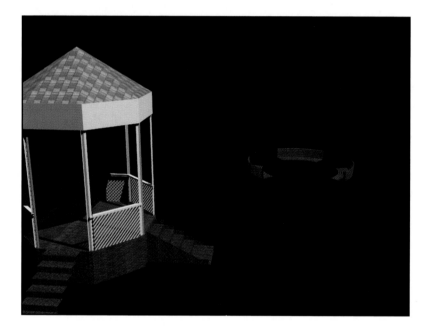

During the course of the following exercises, you create the site, add roads (in this case, paved walkways), vegetation, lighting, man-made items, and atmospheric effects to help add realism to the gazebo project.

Creating a Site

The site for this project has a two-tiered sculpted site with the gazebo and benches sitting on the upper tier and a walkway leading down to the lower tier of the site. The first step is to model the upper tier, the slope, and then the lower tier of the site. The upper and lower tier are considered to be perfectly flat, even though they aren't flat in real life.

Figure 7.2
The gazebo after the exercises.

The Ground

The following exercise shows you how to create the ground of the site for the gazebo. Figure 7.1 shows you the gazebo at the start of this exercise.

1. Choose Create/Box to create the top tier of the site.

2. In the Top viewport, create a box large enough to cover the entire gazebo, as shown in figure 7.3. The box should be fairly thin. Name the object Ground1.

3. Next, verify the position of the ground plane. Make sure that the ground plane falls below the gazebo in the Front viewport. If not, move it into position.

4. Click in the Top viewport to make it the active viewport. Press F1 and switch to the 2D Shaper to create a curved slope.

5. Choose Display/3D Display/On to turn on 3D Display.

6. Choose Display/3D Display/Choose. Select the ground plane by choosing Ground1 from the list.

7. Fit the site to the viewport by using the Zoom Out button to zoom until you can see the complete site.

Figure 7.3

The gazebo with the top tier.

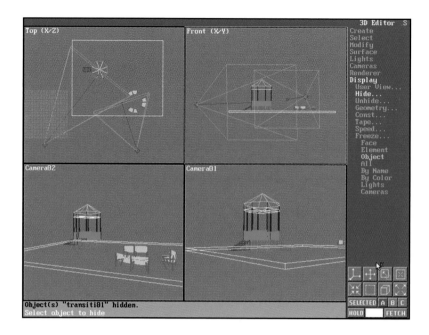

STOP

Zoom extents doesn't work with a 3D display. You will need to use other zoom icons such as zoom out to manipulate the 2D Shaper display.

8. Choose Create/Line to create the outline. Draw a line around the outline of the lower left side of the ground plane, as shown in figure 7.4. Use a snap to make things easier.

9. Make the line a shape by choosing Shape/Assign and selecting the line.

10. Press F2 to switch to the 3D Lofter.

11. Choose Path/Get/Shaper, to get the current shape in the Shaper and use it as the loft path.

12. A warning telling you that you are about to replace the current path appears. Choose OK to this warning.

13. Press F1 to switch back to the Shaper.

14. Now you need to create the profile of the transition between the two tiers of land. Choose Create/Line and create a shape, as shown in figure 7.5. Specify about 4 feet or units for the shape's height.

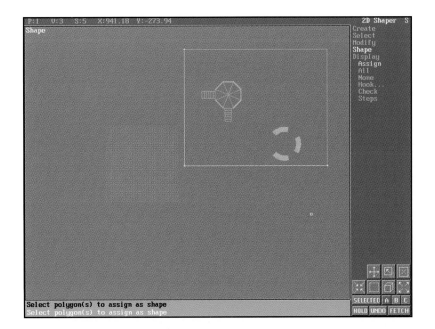

Figure 7.4
The path for the curve.

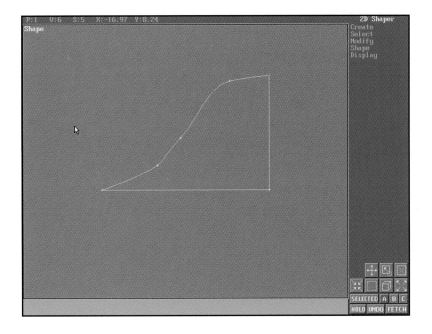

Figure 7.5
*The profile of the transi-
tion.*

15. Set the Hook to the upper left corner, to determine the location of the
loft path.

16. Press F2 to switch to the 3D Lofter.

17. Choose Shapes/Get/Shaper to retrieve the current shape from the Lofter. Figure 7.6 shows you the shape in the Lofter.

Figure 7.6

The profile shape on the loft path.

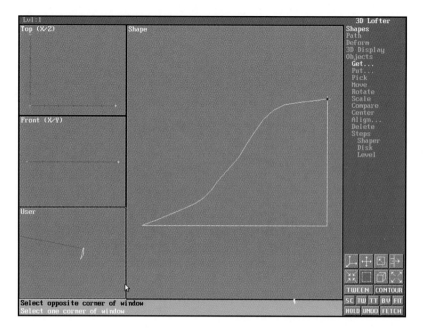

18. Choose Object/Make, so you can loft the object.

19. Name the object Transition. Be sure to turn off Tween, then choose OK to create the transition element.

20. Press F3 to switch to the 3D Editor. The new transition appears in the 3D Editor.

21. Choose Create/Box. Create a box that sits just below the transition element and covers the entire site. Name the box Ground2. Don't worry about overlapping the top and bottom tiers. This creates the bottom tier, as shown in figure 7.7.

The preceding set of steps is just one example of a variety of methods for creating sitework. See the section "Tips and Techniques" later in this chapter for more information on generating random landscapes. Otherwise, explore uses of the Shaper and Lofter to create site elements. Now, you are ready to add a material.

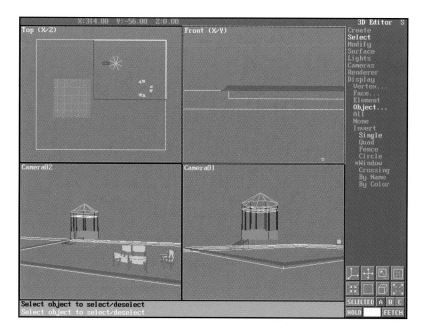

Figure 7.7
The 3D Editor with the second tier.

Find yourself a nice, high-resolution grass image that has a fairly fine grain. You want to map this material to the surface of the site with no tiling. An organic material, such as grass, always shows a repetitive pattern if you tile it. If you don't have a high-resolution material, use Adobe Photoshop and its rubber stamp tool to create a high-resolution material that looks uniform.

1. Press F5 to switch to the Materials Editor. Create the new material, using the settings shown in figure 7.8.

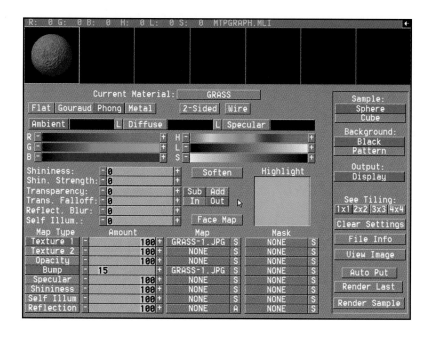

Figure 7.8
The Materials Editor settings for a grass material.

2. Choose File/Put. Save the material to the material library as Grass1.

3. Press F3 to return to the 3D Editor.

4. Choose Surface/Mapping/Type/Planar to specify planar mapping.

5. Align the Mapping icon to the viewport by choosing Surface/Mapping/Adjust/View Align and clicking in the Top viewport.

6. Choose Surface/Mapping/Adjust/Bitmap Fit and select the bitmap you used in the Materials Editor. This makes the Mapping icon proportional to the dimensions of the bitmap.

7. Choose Surface/Mapping/Adjust/Move and center the icon on the site.

8. Choose Surface/Mapping/Adjust/Scale and scale the icon to fit the site, as shown in figure 7.9.

Figure 7.9

The mapping icon on the site.

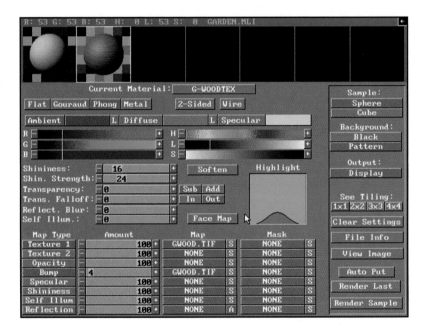

9. Next, apply the mapping to the site. Choose Surface/Mapping/Apply Obj. Apply the mapping to the Ground1, Transition, and Ground2 objects.

10. Assign the grass material to all three objects.

11. Press F1 to switch to the 2D Shaper and save the profile shape as PROFILE.SHP for later use.

At this point, you have assigned the materials and created the basic site. As a sculpted site, creating this site is fairly easy. Other sites might require more extensive use of Modify/Vertex/Move or other commands.

Figure 7.10 shows the rendering of the scene with the new site at this point.

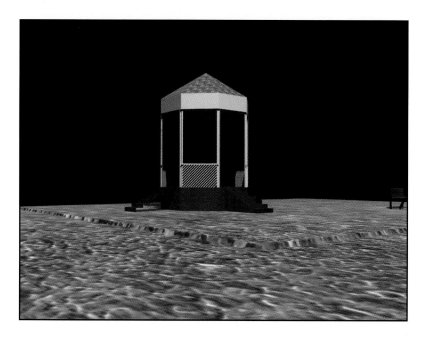

Figure 7.10
The gazebo on the new site.

Roads

Now that you have a site, you're ready to add some walkways to the site. The following steps show how to add a simple walkway. This exercise continues where the last exercise left off.

1. Press F1 to switch to the 2D Shaper.

2. Choose Display/3D Display/On to turn on 3D Display.

3. Choose Display/3D Display/Choose and select all objects in the scene. If the Top viewport isn't active in the 3D Editor, switch back to the 3D Editor and make it active.

4. Create a 2D shape for the walkway, similar to the one shown in figure 7.11. You don't have to be accurate—just approximate it.

5. Assign the polygons as a shape.

6. Switch to the 3D Editor.

7. Choose Create/Object/Get Shape, which enables you to import a 2D shape as a flat object.

8. Name the object Path1 and choose OK, which names and creates the object (see fig. 7.11).

Figure 7.11
The walkway in the 3D Editor.

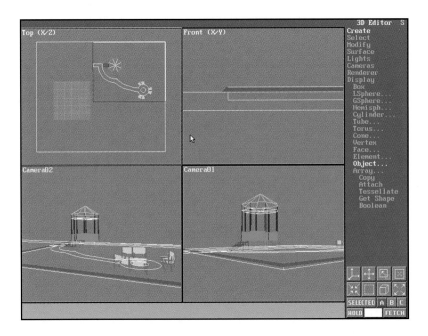

9. In 3D Editor, Front viewport, move the walkway so it's just barely above the ground, which ensures it doesn't overlap the ground.

10. Repeat steps 4–8 to create the second part of the walkway. Figure 7.12 shows the shape. Name the new walkway Path2.

Figure 7.12
The second walkway shape.

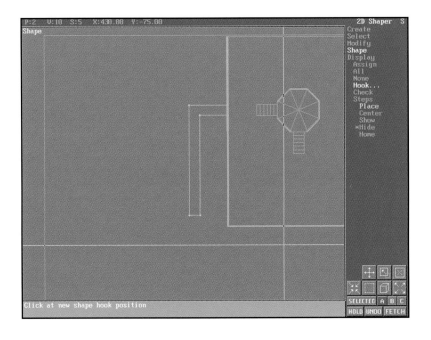

11. In the 3D Editor, Front viewport, move the new walkway into position slightly above the lower ground plane, to ensure that you don't obscure the walkway.

At this point, you have created the walkway for the upper and lower tiers of the site. Now, you need to create the walkway for the transition element. Before you can do this, you must have the shape from the last exercise, PROFILE.SHP.

12. In the 2D Shaper, draw a line segment as shown in figure 7.13. Set this line as the current shape. This line segment becomes a path in the lofter.

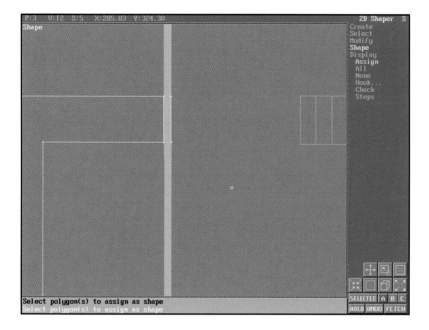

Figure 7.13
The line segment for use as a path.

13. Next, you replace the path in the lofter. Press F2 to switch to the 3D Lofter. Choose Path/Get/Shaper, and choose OK to the Replace Path warning.

14. In the 2D Shaper, load PROFILE.SHP.

15. Switch to the 3D Lofter. Choose Shape/Get/Shaper to load the shape into the lofter.

16. Choose Object/Make and name the object transwalk. Be sure to turn off Tween.

17. In the 3D Editor, position the new walk element as shown in figure 7.14.

Figure 7.14

The new position for the transwalk object.

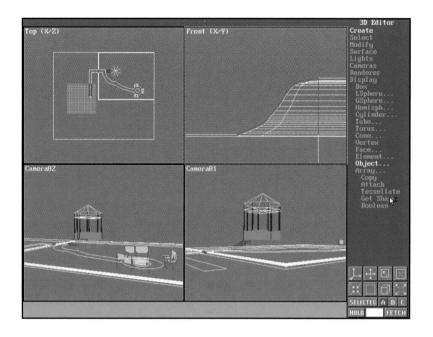

Now, all you have left to do is to create a gravel or asphalt material and apply it to all three objects. Like the grass in the first exercise, you must be careful about tiling the material because you don't want a pattern to show. Use the grass material exercise steps as a guideline for creating the material for the walkway. You might try creating concrete, asphalt, gravel, dirt, and paved walkways.

Now that the site has some walkways, you're ready to add vegetation. You should always add your vegetation after you add your road work, simply because you don't want to accidentally place a tree in the middle of your road.

Vegetation

Next, you add some vegetation to the site. This particular exercise uses both Yost Group's Silicon Garden and 4Dvision's Nursery program. Other techniques are listed in the section "Tips and Techniques" later in this chapter. This exercise takes up where the last exercise left off.

NOTE

The following exercise requires 4D Vision's Nursery IPAS routine. If you do not have this IPAS, you can find similar functionality in Yost Group's Silicon Garden. If you have neither, you should purchase one or both to create trees.

1. Make sure that you're in the 3D Editor.

2. Choose Surface/Material/Get Library, which enables you to load a material library. Nursery has a specific library that you should load before you use the IPAS routine.

3. Select NURSERY.MLI from the list to load the NURSERY.MLI library.

4. Choose Program/PXP Loader and select Nursery from the list to opens the Nursery dialog box (see fig. 7.15).

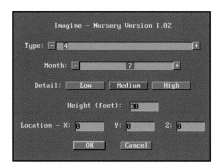

Figure 7.15
The Nursery dialog box.

Nursery uses numbers to refer to each of the tree types it can create. 4Dvision furnishes a poster that shows each tree number.

5. Set the Type to number 25 and the detail to Low.

6. Set the location of the tree to 428',0,98'. This location will vary depending on where you want to create the tree, and the measurement assumes you use architectural units.

7. Choose OK to generate the tree (see fig. 7.16).

Owing to some inconsistencies in the Nursery program, you might need to rescale the tree to get the correct scale. It depends on your unit setting. If you work in architectural units, you probably need to scale the tree up 400%, then by 300% again to get the tree to the correct size, as shown in figure 7.16.

8. Choose Select/Object/Quad and select all objects in the tree.

9. Choose Modify/Object/Move and choose the Select button, which enables you to move the selected objects.

10. Hold down the Shift key and move the tree to a new location to make a clone. When you choose the new location, a dialog box appears.

Figure 7.16

The gazebo with the first tree.

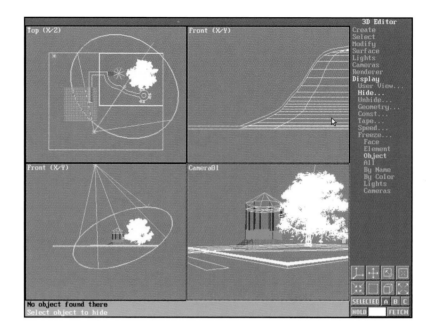

11. Choose Multiple in the Copy to dialog box that appears. This enables you to create copies of all the objects. Note that you must create many new object names. Figure 7.17 shows the rendering of the gazebo with two trees.

Figure 7.17

The gazebo with two trees.

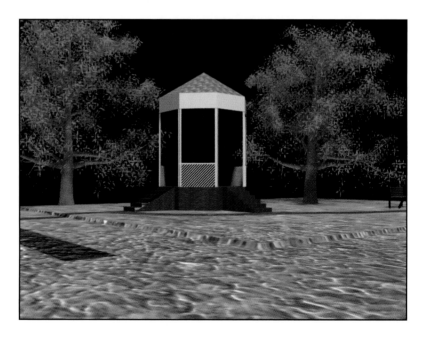

Nursery trees are highly detailed 3D objects. In the previous section of the exercise, the file size of the model was 245 KB at the start of the exercise. Adding the second nursery tree increased the file size to 4.8 MB. Make sure that you have enough RAM to be able to handle the size of the Nursery trees. As you can see, you should use no more than you absolutely must.

The next couple steps in the exercise entail using Yost Group's Silicon Garden routine to add additional vegetation elements. Silicon Garden also creates trees. Here, you use Silicon Garden to add some flowers along the path of the walkway.

12. Choose Surface/Material/Get Library to load a material library. Like Nursery, Silicon Garden has its own material library. Select GARDEN.MLI.

13. Press F12 or choose Program/PXP Loader, which enables you to load a PXP routine. Select SG (for Silicon Garden).

14. Choose OK to load the routine. Figure 7.18 shows the resulting dialog box.

Figure 7.18
The Silicon Garden dialog box.

15. Choose Flowers, then OK, to select the vegetation type, Flower, and open the flowers dialog box (see fig. 7.19).

Figure 7.19
The Silicon Garden - Flowers dialog box.

16. Choose Rose, then OK, to select the flower type, Rose, and open the Rose dialog box (see fig. 7.20).

17. Set the Age to 21 and specify Yellow as the color, then choose OK to create the flower according to these parameters. The flower is created at 0,0,0.

Figure 7.20

The Silicon Garden: Rose dialog box.

Select the flower and position it. Then choose Modify/Move and clone the flower to make copies. Figure 7.21 shows the rendering of the gazebo with several flowers. Simply repeat the Silicon Garden routine to add as much vegetation as you need—but keep an eye on your file size, for it grows rapidly.

Figure 7.21

The gazebo with the flowers.

At this point, you just add more vegetation until you're satisfied with the image. See the section "Tips and Techniques" later in this chapter for methods on reducing your face count and keeping your file size under control when it comes to vegetation and large trees.

Man-Made Items

After you add vegetation to your site, you're ready to add some man-made items. In the next exercise, you add a fountain to the center of the ring of benches. You could add other items at your discretion. This exercise picks up where the last exercise left off.

1. Go to the 2D Shaper to create the outline. Draw a squiggly shape, similar to the one shown in figure 7.22. Place the hook as shown in the figure as well. Make the shape no taller than 4'.

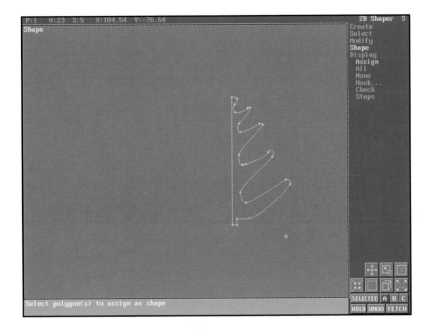

Figure 7.22
The fountain shape.

2. Press F2 and switch to the Lofter.

3. Choose Path/SurfRev to create a circular path.

4. Set the diameter to 4' and choose OK, then choose OK again in response to the warning message.

5. Choose Shape/Get/Shaper to load the shape from the Shaper. Figure 7.23 shows the Lofter with the path and shape loaded.

6. Choose Object/Make. Name the object FOUNTAIN and turn on Tween, then choose OK to create the fountain.

7. Position the fountain at the center of the circular walkway around the benches.

8. Assign Blue marble to the material and assign cylindrical mapping to the fountain. Figure 7.24 shows the resulting fountain.

For an on-your-own type of exercise, see if you can add water to the fountain or add a spray to the top of the fountain. Now, you can simply create any other man-made items for the site that you might need. In this case, the benches are man-made items (they were created earlier so you could create the walkways correctly).

Figure 7.23
The 3D Lofter with the shape and path.

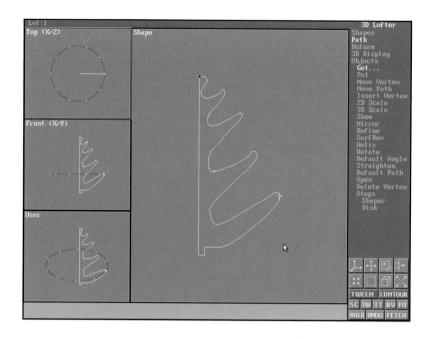

Figure 7.24
The rendered fountain in the scene.

After you add the man-made items, you might want or need to go back and add more vegetation around the man-made items. You might, for example, add some more flowers or shrubs around the fountain.

Skies and Backgrounds

The following exercises show you how to add two types of skies to your scene, one as background, and one as a static sphere. The first exercise demonstrates a regular perspective matched background.

1. In the 3D Editor, activate the Camera01 viewport.

2. Choose Renderer/Setup/Background, which enables you to set up a background image and opens a dialog box (see fig. 7.25).

Figure 7.25
The Background Method dialog box.

3. Choose Bitmap and then click on the blank box next to the bitmap button.

4. Choose Lake2.TGA and then OK to select the bitmap for use.

> **At this point, you can use any bitmap file as a background. For a specific background, you can take a photograph of the site and scan it. Just make sure that the bitmap image is the same size as the output rendering resolution, to save memory and time in the rendering process.**

NOTE

5. Choose OK to return to the 3D Editor.

6. Choose Program/Camera/Prevu or press F7 to load the fast preview module.

7. Choose Horizon. Adjust the perspective of the image until it matches the horizon line, as shown in figure 7.26.

8. After you adjust the perspective, choose Exit to exit the fast preview module.

9. Choose OK to update the camera. This adjusts the camera position to match the image. Figure 7.27 shows you the rendered image.

Figure 7.26

The fast preview with horizon line.

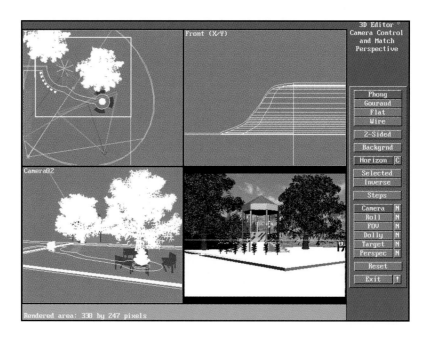

Figure 7.27

The gazebo with a background.

The preceding methods works great with still images, but not with animations. You can use an animated bitmap, such as a FLI file or an IFL (Image File List), to produce animated backgrounds. Keeping the perspective correct across time, however, proves very difficult. The next part shows you how to create a different type of background—a sphere-based sky—that you can animate rather easily, but not perspective match.

1. In the 3D Editor, choose Zoom Extents in the Top viewport to maximize the view of the Top viewport.

2. Choose Create/Hemisphere/Smoothed. Create the hemisphere in the Top viewport so that it's large enough to cover all objects, as shown in figure 7.28. Name the object SKY.

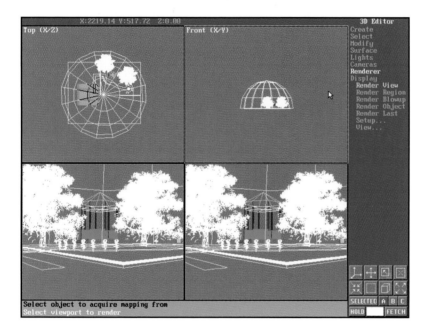

Figure 7.28
The hemisphere.

3. Choose Surface/Normals/Object Flip and select the hemisphere. This flips the normals of the hemisphere to the interior, so the bitmap renders on the correct side.

4. Choose Surface/Mapping/Type and select Spherical.

5. Choose Surface/Mapping/Adjust/Center and select the hemisphere. This centers the mapping icon to the center of the hemisphere.

6. Choose Surface/Mapping/Adjust/Move and move the mapping icon to match the sphere in the Front viewport. This corrects the mapping icon to match a hemisphere rather than a sphere.

7. Choose Surface/Mapping/Adjust/Rotate and rotate the mapping icon to match figure 7.29. This rotates the mapping icon so the seams of the bitmap don't show in the camera view. You should always try to keep the seams behind the camera.

Figure 7.29

The mapping icon rotated.

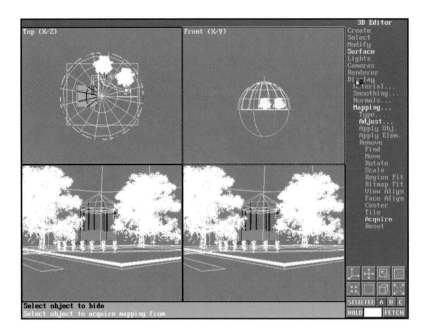

8. Choose Surface/Mapping/Apply Obj and select the hemisphere to apply the mapping coordinates to the hemisphere.

9. Create a material using any sky bitmap as the texture 1 map. Apply this material to the hemisphere and render. The scene should come out a lot like figure 7.30.

As you can see, you can use different methods to create the sky. The question is whether you intend to animate the scene.

Figure 7.30
The gazebo with a hemi-sphere sky.

Tips and Techniques

The following are some brief tips and techniques related to creating various landscaping objects.

◆ You can use Vista Pro (A DOS program) to create fractal and random landscapes. This is great for creating landscapes for games or other types of animations.

◆ You can use Yost Group's Displace IPAS routine to displace a mesh into a 3D landscape. Depending on the bitmap you choose, this can produce some very nice effects.

◆ When dealing with real trees in your scene. Populate the front of the scene with 3D trees. In the back of the scene, use flat 3D faces with opacity mapped trees. You can create the opacity maps simply by rendering an elevation of the real tree. Then, take the rendering image and invert it in Photoshop. With a little practice, you can create a tree with only four or six faces. Use crossing faces to create flat trees that look more realistic.

◆ Use IPAS routines to create effects such as waves on water.

◆ Use animated texture maps for complex effects such as moving rivers or streams in your site.

◆ Populate your exterior with people and cars when necessary to give a good sense of scale to the scene.

Summary

Based on the exercises in this chapter, you can see that creating landscaping can be plenty of fun, but also a substantial amount of work. As you create landscapes, you should be aware of the file sizes that you generate, for they get large quite quickly.

When dealing with outdoor landscaping, you will probably find yourself resorting to IPAS routines quite frequently. If you ever try to model a tree, you know why. When you compose a scene, just be sure not to overuse the IPAS routines and add too much vegetation. You need to strike a balance between too much and too little in the overall landscape, so as not to detract from the building that sits on the site.

Creating a Demo Reel

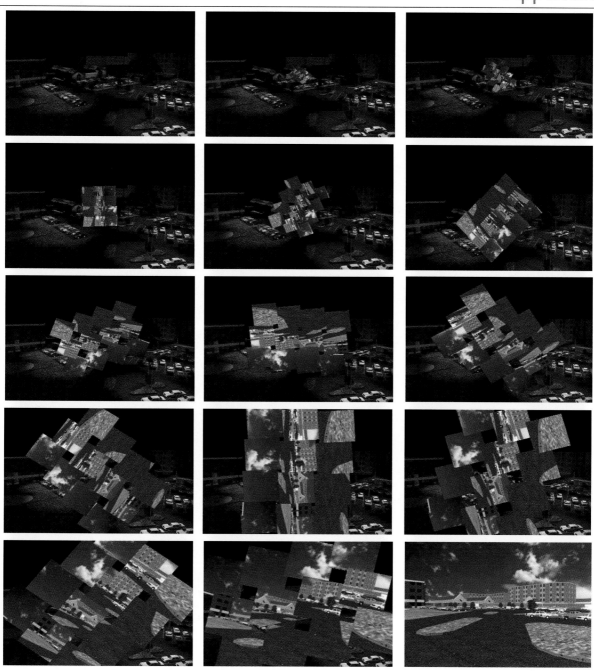

by Todd Peterson
Knoxville, Tennessee

Author Bio

Todd is the owner of MTP Graphics, an architectural rendering, animation, multimedia, and training company located in Knoxville, Tennessee. When he is not rendering and animating to his heart's content, he spends time teaching AutoCAD and 3D Studio at Pellissippi State Community College. In the past, Todd has also taught at the University of Tennessee College of Architecture. Additionally, Todd has authored other titles for New Riders Publishing, including *3D Studio for Beginners*, *Windows NT for Graphics Professionals*, and the *AutoCAD Performance Tuning Toolkit*.

Chapter Overview

The business world today is extremely competitive. You need to take advantage of every opportunity you get to become successful. When it comes to rendering and animation, one of the ways you can be competitive is to produce an exciting and well-done demonstration reel.

You can then distribute this reel to prospective clients and existing clients on VHS or higher-quality video tape. When the clients view the tape, they get an excellent opportunity to compare the quality of work you can produce for them against what other companies can offer. Whether your work is rendering and animation or architectural design, a demo reel is the best method for showing off your skills.

This chapter focuses on the techniques, skills, hardware, and software you need to create an effective demo reel of your work. This chapter focuses on the following topics:

- Components of a demo reel

- Hardware you need to create the reel

- Software you need to create the reel

- Designing the demo reel

- Creating the demo reel

- Creating the reel labels

Components of a Demo Reel

A *demo reel* is a compilation of your or a company's best work for distribution on VHS video tape. This demo reel usually is a fast-paced synopsis of current and past work, synchronized to sound.

A demo reel includes a variety of different components, depending on how you design your demo reel and what you try to say with it. You run across the following demo reel components more often than most:

- Animation

- Still images

- Sound

- Transitions

- Special effects

- Titles

- Text

Animation is the main component of a demo reel. Most artists try to keep the animation segments on a demo reel fairly short and in rapid succession in an attempt to keep the viewer's interest. In general, an artist tries to keep the animation segments to between 3 and 6 seconds long. For architectural work, however, 3 to 6 seconds often isn't long enough for full comprehension of the work.

Still imagery is something many people don't normally think of as part of a demo reel. In architectural work, however, the still image is a powerful way to convey design intent, visualization quality, or mood. Combining segments of animation and still imagery lets your client get a good sense of the variety of work you do. A still image also gives the client a better opportunity to pause the video tape player to take a longer look at the work.

Sound is another key component of a successful demo reel. Have you ever noticed how some of the greatest motion pictures always had some sort of background sound? Take, for example, *Star Wars*. Every second of that movie has some sort of background music. A demo reel isn't all that different. You can use sounds and music to help dictate pace, set a sense of mood or excitement, or to signal key events in your video reel. The exact type, style, or beat of music that you choose should be a combination of the type of music that you like and the type of music that the pace of the demo reel requires. You wouldn't use Metallica, for example, for a walk through a garden; George Winston might be more appropriate in this case.

Transitions are an important aspect of demo reels as well. A *transition* is a way to smoothly change one image to another in the demo reel. If you're watching a walkthrough of a house, and suddenly a walkthrough of a hospital appears, you have created a poor transition. A better transition might be to have the house animation fade out to black, then have the hospital animation fade in from black, as one example of hundreds of other types of transitions you can create and use to provide variety in your work.

Special effects are a handy component of a demo reel. A *special effect* is any type of effect considered out of the ordinary. You could use a variety of special IPAS routines in your animation to create unique special effects. Or you could use other types of special effects, such as pixelating frames or warping and twisting a frame. It all depends on the type of mood and character you want in your animation.

Titles, and titling in general, are important for a demo reel. The most important reason to use titling is to tell viewers who you are. You also can use titles to divide segments of the animation or to add additional special effects. You can animate most titles over time to make them more interesting.

Similar to titles and titling is text. You use text in a demo reel simply to provide information, such as descriptions about services or products you're selling or providing. The key to using text is to make sure viewers can read it (it needs to be big enough and needs to stay on-screen long enough).

By combining one or more of these components, you can create an exciting, high-quality demo reel that conveys your message to your clients or prospective clients.

Hardware Needed To Create the Reel

Before you begin to design your demo reel, you should be aware of the hardware you need to create the demo reel. Some of the most common hardware options include:

- Par and Perception boards

- Tape decks

- Editing decks

- Soundboards

Par and Perception Boards

The Par and Perception boards are two types of special video compression boards designed specifically to work with 3D Studio for the explicit purpose of providing an inexpensive but high-quality method for recording animation to video tape. The Perception board is a newer version of the Par board and has slightly higher quality output. Both boards are heavily used by all types of 3D Studio animators. Hence, the Par and Perception boards are some of the most popular solutions for these problems today.

NOTE

> **The techniques described in this chapter are based on techniques for which you would use a Par or Perception board, although you can adopt other equipment to these techniques.**

Digital Processing Systems (DPS) makes both the Par and Perception boards. The Par and Perception boards both use a proprietary Motion JPEG compression scheme to convert individual Targa images to their proprietary ANI animation file format. The Perception board is intended for use under

Windows 95 and Windows NT. Under those environments, the Perception board has a unique file system that makes the ANI file appear as sequences of Targas, TIFFs, BMPs, or other file formats.

Table A.1 shows you the features of the Par and the Perception boards.

Table A.1	Features of the Par and Perception Boards	
Feature	*Par*	*Perception*
Drive	Enhanced IDE	SCSI-2
Maximum capacity storage animation (times depend on compression ratios)	2.6 GB (2 drives) 18 to 25 minutes	63 GB (7 drives) 2 to 3 hours
Output	Composite, SVHS, Betacam SP	Composite, SVHS, Betacam SP
Input file type	Targa	Targa
Input file res.	752×480	720×480
Output file type	ANI, STL	ANI, STL, TIFF, TARGA, BMP, IFF
BUS slot type	Full Length ISA	Full Length PCI
Playback speed	30 FPS, 60 Fields	30 FPS, 60 Fields

Both the Par and Perception boards provide some unique capabilities. Both work with most nonlinear video editing software. Both allow you to add and remove single frames from an animation—a handy feature if you want change just a couple of frames. The Par board works directly with 3D Studio and offers a PXP IPAS routine that enables you to record directly to the Par drive. The Perception board works with 3D Studio MAX and other Windows NT- or Windows 95-based animation software. You can copy 3D Studio DOS files to the Perception board after you render them, as well. Figure A.1 shows the Par board's PXP routine interface running inside 3D Studio.

The Par board also provides DOS-based and Windows NT-based controller programs. Figure A.2 shows the DOS-based program and figure A.3 shows the NT-based program.

The relative cost of a Par or Perception board setup is about $1,500 to $1,800, not including the dedicated hard drive. The cost of the hard drive depends on the size of the hard drive you want to use. Generally, the hard drives run anywhere from $300 to $2,400. The Par and Perception boards output to D1 video quality when you use a Betacam SP deck. Providing D1 quality in this price range makes a Par or Perception board a great low-cost solution when compared to that of a still frame VTR subsystm as described in the next section.

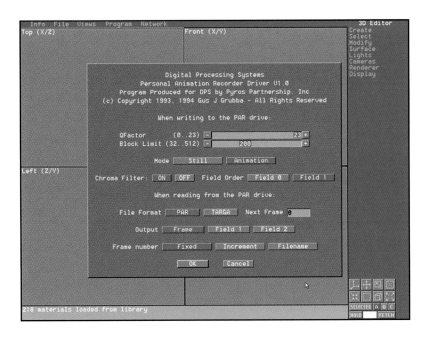

Figure A.1
The Par driver running in 3D Studio.

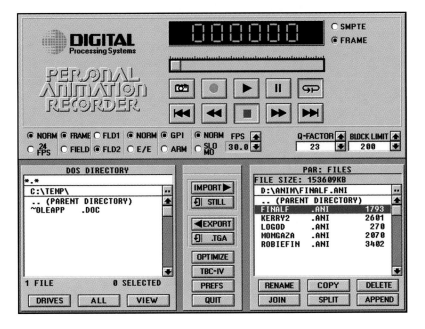

Figure A.2
The Par 1.51 driver software for DOS.

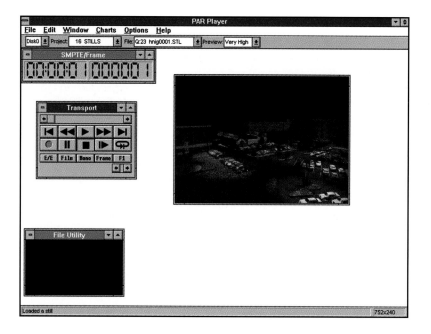

VTR or VCR

You must have a VCR or VTR before you can create a demo reel. A VCR is a standard off-the-shelf video recorder you can buy at any electronics store. A VTR is a video tape recorder, a special type of video recorder you can use a computer to control.

If you use a Par or Perception board, you can effectively record to VHS (composite) or SVHS VCRs. The Par and Perception boards also work with SVHS and Betacam SP VTRs. The difference between the three is the overall quality. Betacam SP provides the highest quality and playback resolution. SVHS provides over 400 lines of resolution, or about twice the resolution of a VHS deck.

For general distribution of demo reels, a VHS VCR is adequate. For broadcast on TV, Betacam SP is the minimum. SVHS falls somewhere in between. Just remember that you can't play an SVHS tape in a VHS VCR, and you want to record to whatever type of device your client or prospective client can use.

Editing Decks

The other option besides a Par or Perception board is to use a video tape deck editing suite, usually two or more SVHS or higher-quality video decks with advanced video compositing functions. These VTRs start at about $5,000 per VTR, so this solution starts at $15,000.

Using an editing deck and single-frame recording is a higher-quality solution than using a Par or Perception board, but as you can see, you do pay a pretty price for it. In general, if you are creating the animation for broadcast on TV, an editing deck is best. Otherwise, a Par or Perception board provides more than enough quality for architectural work. The editing decks take much longer to use. Nonlinear editing software cannot use them. You spend considerable amounts of time recording segments of animation from one VTR to another, sometimes adding simple transitions—a long and tedious process.

Sound Boards

The last piece of hardware that you need is a good 16-bit sound card. A Soundblaster 16 by Creative Labs is a minimum sound card for use in recording sound to a video tape. Recording 16-bit sound at 44 KHz results in CD-quality sound. If you want the highest-quality sound on your demo tape, you need to record it at 16-bit, 44 KHz, which produces very large sound files (roughly 50 MB per minute of sound).

Any of a variety of sound cards can serve this type of purpose. If you can, go with Turtle Beach's Multisound Monterey sound card, which contains special hardware for recording and digitized sound. The Monterey card provides exceptional playback. It also supports MIDI and wavetable synthesis, which gives you a variety of musical options.

TIP

If you can't afford the hardware just discussed, some service bureaus have studios that provide some or all of the necessary hardware. You can explore those options, but if you do, you'll probably find yourself spending almost as much in studio fees as you would just going ahead and purchasing a Perception or Par board and drive.

Software Needed To Create the Reel

After you have the hardware in place to create the demo reel, you probably want or need to use some additional software outside of 3D Studio. All the necessary software is Windows-based and runs on Windows 3.11, 95, or NT.

You basically need several types of software packages. The following list briefly describes each of these types:

◆ **Nonlinear Video Editor.** Lets you edit a series of images, an AVI, or other format file. Called *nonlinear* because you can cut and paste the animation at any point, synchronize sound, and add transitions and other effects.

◆ **Image Editor.** Enables you to edit (such as resize, retouch, adjust, and manipulate) any still image.

◆ **Sound Editor.** Enables you to edit and work with sound files.

In:Sync's Razor Pro

In:Sync's Razor Pro (see fig. A.4) is one of the leading nonlinear editing packages. It offers several distinct features, all briefly described in the following list:

Figure A.4
Razor Pro 1.0F Editor.

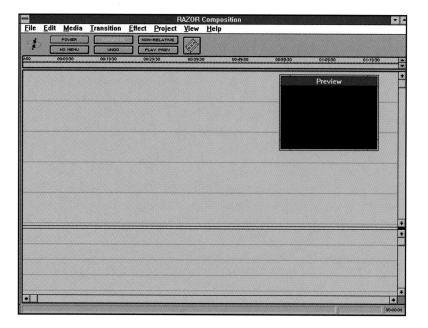

♦ **Media Library.** A single interface to view all the different types of media that Razor Pro supports, including stills, animations, sound, effects, and transitions. Figure A.5 shows you a typical media library interface.

♦ **Unlimited channels.** A channel is a location in which you can put a segment of animation, sounds, transitions, or effects. You place them on a time line so they are easy to synchronize. Figure A.6 shows you the Razor Editor with several channels loaded, including an audio track.

♦ **The capability to work with Par files.** Razor Pro is the only nonlinear editor that can work directly with the Par's native file format. Others must convert the ANI file format to some other format before they can use it.

Overall, Razor Pro is a fast and efficient nonlinear editor. It has a considerably faster older brother, named Speed Razor Mach III, that runs only on Windows NT. If you were to use a Perception board and have Windows NT, you would choose Speed Razor over Razor Pro. Aside from speed and Speed Razor's NT limitation, the brothers are basically identical, supporting the same interface and features.

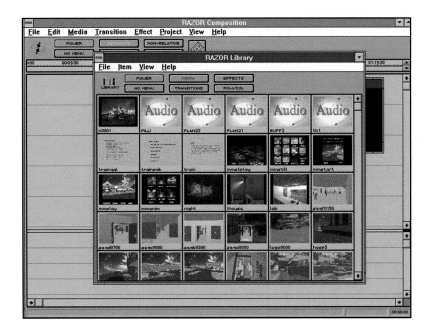

Figure A.5
The Razor Pro Media Library.

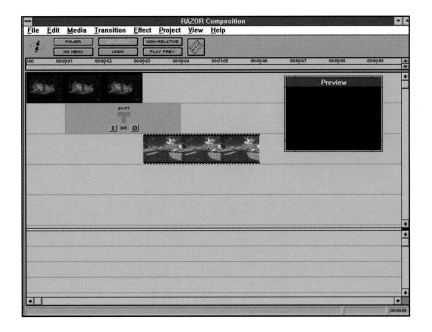

Figure A.6
Razor Pro with a few tracks.

Adobe Premiere

Adobe Premiere is the leading nonlinear video editor. Although its original purpose was to work mostly with AVI files, you can use it to edit sequences of Targa files generated from 3D studio. Premiere can handle Par files by using a DPS-furnished ANI-to-AVI converter that runs under Windows 3.1. Figure A.7 shows the Adobe Premiere interface.

Figure A.7

The Adobe Premiere 4.0 interface.

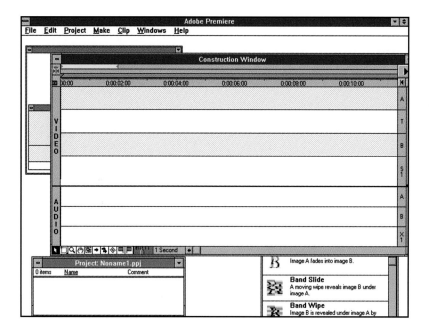

Like Razor Pro, Premiere has several distinct features, briefly described in the following list:

◆ **Animated transitions.** Adobe Premiere's Transitions dialog box (see fig. A.8) provides you with quick sample animations of each of its transitions.

Figure A.8

The Adobe Premiere Transitions dialog box.

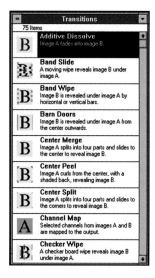

◆ **Support for Photoshop plug-ins.** Since Adobe also makes Photoshop, Premiere offers excellent support for all Adobe Photoshop plug-ins, providing you with a wealth of special effects.

◆ **Separated channels.** Unlike Razor, Premiere offers separate channels for audio, video, and transitions and effects, which keeps the interface more organized. Figure A.9 shows the Construction Window. The channels covered with slanted gray lines are the video or animation channels.

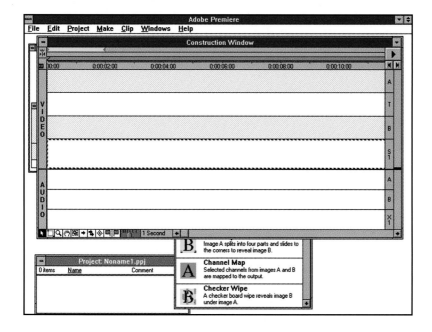

Figure A.9
Premiere's Construction Window.

To create your demo reel, you should use Adobe Premiere or Razor Pro. Both are equally capable of enabling you to create and composite your video tape. Adobe Premiere is used for the purposes of this chapter.

Elastic Reality's Transjammer

Elastic Reality is a company that specializes in special effects. Their Transjammer package is a set of 60 or so specialized transitions. You can use these transitions inside of Premiere or Razor Pro, and they provide a great degree of flexibility.

If you want the most options for your demo reel, you should pick up this package to work in conjunction with Premiere or Razor Pro. The additional transitions appear in Premiere's Transitions dialog box or Razor Pro's Media Library.

Adobe Photoshop

Another mandatory piece of software is Adobe Photoshop. If you don't already use Photoshop to touch up your renderings, you should. Photoshop is the most advanced image-editing package available for Windows. You can use it to correct any rendering error, as well as to add special effects, such as lens flares. Figure A.10 shows the Photoshop interface.

Figure A.10

The Adobe Photoshop 3.04 interface.

As you can see, you need plenty of hardware and software before you can create demo reels in-house. When you consider that you will probably make *at least* one demo reel per year, the cost doesn't seem so prohibitive compared to that of a service bureau.

Designing the Demo Reel

Before you actually create your demo reel, you should design it. Your first step should be to create a *storyboard*, a series of simple sketches outlining the flow of the overall animation. As an animator, you're probably familiar with storyboarding. During storyboarding, you should consider several factors when you design your demo reel, including the following:

♦ Excitement

♦ Timing

- ◆ Sound

- ◆ Transitions

- ◆ Text

Excitement

Every demo reel should have some degree of excitement. The more exciting your demo reel, the better your likely response to it. You can evoke excitement in several ways:

- ◆ **Pace.** A quick pace makes your demo reel more exciting. You can keep a quick pace by using short segments of animations or stills. Just make sure you give the viewer enough time to see the animations and stills; otherwise, the viewer loses interest. Generally speaking, 3 seconds should be a minimum length of time for viewing an animation segment or still, and 5 or 6 seconds is a comfortable amount of time.

- ◆ **Sound.** Sound is key to the excitement of a demo reel. A lively soundtrack automatically excites the viewers—unless they don't like the music. You should try to choose upbeat but fairly neutral music.

- ◆ **Special effects.** Adding special effects, such as explosions, lens flares, transitions, and so on, creates a more exciting demo reel. Architecture rarely ever explodes, but you could have titles between your buildings explode, melt, or catch on fire.

Basically, do whatever you think you can to evoke excitement in the demo reel. Just don't take it to the point where you offend your viewers, because then you just lose them.

Timing

Timing in a demo reel also is critical. If you have a bouncing ball in your demo reel, for example, you need the sound to be synchronized to it perfectly to achieve the effect you want.

Timing also affects the order in which you present your information. You might decide you want a variety of building types in your demo reel, including libraries, jails, schools, malls, renovations, and so on. A jail, for example, has many restrictions on decor and lighting, which has a tendency to reduce the overall impact of a jail animation sequence. On the other hand, a school, church, or other such building type provides you with a variety of opportunities for lighting material and texture that provide a more interesting animation sequence. When you compose the reel, you should try to intermix less interesting segments with more interesting segments, to help keep the viewer on a fairly even keel.

Sound

As mentioned earlier, sound is very important to the demo reel. As you plan your demo reel, you should consider the types of sounds you want. Sound is very powerful at evoking moods, so the type of sound you choose for a particular segment of the demo reel becomes very important.

Sound makes a huge difference in the quality of a demo reel. Even if you can't find the right sounds or get them synchronized correctly, make sure you have some sort of sound throughout your entire demo—you'll get a much better response if you do.

Transitions

Transitions are important when you switch animations or stills in the demo tape. Both Premiere and Razor Pro, combined with Transjammer, provide nearly 100 different types of transitions. Depending on the type of demo reel you create, you should use a few selected transitions for consistency, or go all out and use as many different transitions as you can. Figure A.11 shows a still image in the middle of a swirl transition.

Figure A.11

An image with a swirl transition.

Text

The last thing to think about when you design the demo reel is how you use text in titling or information screens. Try to keep text usage down to a minimum (like down to not at all) in a demo reel. Most people watch the demo reel for visual stimulation, not to read. Send an accompanying brochure before you use lots of text in a demo reel. If you must have text in the reel, use it only for titles of the various sections of your demo reel.

TIP

Creating the Demo Reel

Creating the demo reel can be broken down into several distinct steps. The following list isolates and briefly describes each step:

1. Create the individual animation, still, text, and other sequences you want to include in the demo reel. You can use digital video, Par, or still image formats for these segments.

2. Use a nonlinear time editor to sequence the steps. You also should add your transitions during this phase.

3. Create and sequence the sound for the animation. You can apply sound in small segments too, just like animation segments.

4. Preview the animation with sound. If it meets your expectations, move to the next step; otherwise, correct any errors you find.

5. Have the nonlinear editing software render the entire demo reel sequence to either individual Targa files or to your Par or Perception card hard drive.

6. Record the animation to a master video tape.

More detailed information about how to create a demo reel using Adobe Premiere and a Par board setup can be found on the New Riders Web site at http://www.mcp.com/newriders/.

NOTE

Summary

As you can see, creating a demo reel requires some specific hardware and software, and plenty of time. Your choice of hardware and software can make a great difference in how easy or how hard creating the demo reel is for you. The preferred choices are as follows:

◆ DPS's Perception Board with a 4 GB drive

◆ In:Sync's Speed Razor running on NT

- ◆ Turtle Beach's Multisound Monterey Card

- ◆ An SHVS VCR and a VHS VCR to create masters and duplicates

With this setup, you can create just about any demo video tape. The length of the video tape is restricted only by the amount of drive space on the Perception card.

Above all, be as creative and imaginative as you can in the creation of your demo reel. Remember, you're making this reel to show off to prospective clients, or to enter into competitions. Your work on this reel should be your best work possible. Try to make the reel as exciting and innovative as you can, and you will get a great response from it.

Index

Symbols

D

DDOSNAP command, inserting drawing files, 14
DDUCSP command, creating UCS settings, 18
Delete command
    Omni lights, 159
    spotlights, 164
Demo reel, 231-232
    animations, 232
    creating, 245
    designing storyboards, 242
    editing decks, 236
    editors
        image, 237
        nonlinear video, 237
        sound, 237
    Par boards, 233-234
    Perception boards, 233-234
    software, 237
    sound boards, 237
    sounds, 232, 243-244
    special effects, 232, 243
    text, 233, 244
    timing, 243
    titles, 233
    transitions, 232, 244
    VCR, 236
    VTR, 236
designing demo reel storyboards, 242
DFXOUT command, importing objects into 3D
  studio, 12
dialog boxes
    Viewpoint Presets, 24
    Alpha, 87
    Camera Definition, 129
    Keyboard Step Rate, 189
    Local Shadow Control, 165
    Mapping Coordinates, 63
    Mapping Parameters, 61, 85
    Omni Light Definition, 158
    Queue Entry, 86
    Shadow Map Control, 94
    Spotlight Definition, 162
    UCS Orientation, 18
digital cameras, creating texture libraries, 57
Displace (IPAS routine), 227
Display/Hide command, rendering objects, 119

DISTANCE command, viewing 3D models, 21
DIVIDE command, creating models, 43
Dolly command, spotlights, 164, 192
domes, creating backgrounds, 135
DOOR01 layer, 11
DOOR02 layer, 11
drawing files
    creating, 13
    inserting Xrefs, 13
    viewing in 3D, 14
drive-bys (animation), 133
dusk scenes, lighting, 171
DVIEW command, 16
    viewing 3D models, 20
DXF files
    converting to 3DS, 43
    loading/merging, 42
DXF3DS.EXE, converting DXF files to 3DS, 43
DXFOUT command, importing AutoCAD
  models, 37

E

Ease To/From spinners, creating motion in animations, 99
editing decks, 236
editors
    3D Editor, 184
    image editor, 237
    nonlinear video editor, 237
    nonlinear video editors, Adobe Premiere, 239-
      241
    sound editor, 237
effects lighting, 92
elevations, viewing Front, 25-26
Entity option, loading/merging DXF files, 42
environment maps, animation, 84-85
environments, 3D modeling, 18
exporting 3DS files to AutoCAD, 43-44
exterior models
    creating
      file size considerations, 111
      selecting materials, 113
    planning, 109-110
EXTRUDE command, creating models, 29
extruding lines, 26-27
    creating models, 28

F

faces, 27
   flipping, 43
   missing, importing CAD files into 3D Studio, 149
   segmented, creating models, 43
fading animations, 104
Falloff command, spotlights, 164
fencing textures, opacity mapping, 66-68
Field of View (FOV), 191
field rendering, animations, 102
File menu commands, New, 13
files
   3D drawings, creating, 13
   animation file types, 225
   animations, IFL files, 88
   converting DXF to 3DS, 43
   DFX, importing objects into 3D Studio, 12
   drawing, viewing in 3D, 14
   format, animations, 103
   importing
      assigning materials, 151
      planning, 150-151
   inserting drawing files, 13-14
   loading/merging, 42
   saving, DXF format, 43-44
   size considerations, exterior models, 111
   solid models, size considerations, 11
   virtual memory swap files, 71
Filmroll option, importing AutoCADmodels, 38
fixtures, adding to interior models, 82
Flat view, 189
flipping faces, 43
floor plans, Xrefs
   creating 3D floor plans, 13
Fly-bys
   animation, 133
      backgrounds, 135
      creating, 136-143
fountains, landscaping sites, 220-221
FOV (Field of View), 191
fractals, landscaping sites, 227
frame rendering, animations, 102
frit patterns, 109
front elevation, viewing, 25-26
furnishings, adding to interior models, 82
furniture libraries, 82

G

gamma animations, 103-104
glass, 185
   in models, 29
   single panes, 36-37
GLAZ01 layer, 37
glazing (glass), 116-117
   creating in models, 29, 36
Gouraud view, 189
grass, landscaping sites, 211-213
ground, landscaping sites, 207-210

H

hardware (demo reel)
   editing decks, 236
   Par boards, 234
   Perception boards, 234
   sound boards, 237
   VCR, 236
   VTR, 236
Hidden line command, 10
HIDE command
   creating perspective views, 17
   hiding lines in 3D models, 22
hiding objects, 189
high resolution images
   rendering, 132, 197-198
   screen resolution, 132
highlights (Shin. Strength), 152
horizon lines, 188
   locating, 190-191
Hotspot command, spotlights, 164

I

IFL files, animations, 88
Image CELS texture library, 56
Image editor, 237
images
   combining, 196-197
   high resolution
      rendering, 132, 197-198
      screen resolution, 132
   outputting, 198
   printing, 198-200

Q-R

S

T

Check Us Out Online!

New Riders has emerged as a premier publisher of computer books for the professional computer user. Focusing on CAD/graphics/multimedia, communications/internetworking, and networking/operating systems, New Riders continues to provide expert advice on high-end topics and software.

Check out the online version of *New Riders' Official World Wide Web Yellow Pages, 1996 Edition* for the most engaging, entertaining, and informative sites on the Web! You can even add your own site!

*Hind Fire
Copyright 1995 - John Brooks*

Brave our site for the finest collection of CAD and 3D imagery produced today. Professionals from all over the world contribute to our gallery, which features new designs every month.

From Novell to Microsoft, New Riders publishes the training guides you need to attain your certification. Visit our site and try your hand at the CNE Endeavor, a test engine created by VFX Technologies, Inc. that enables you to measure what you know—and what you don't!

New Riders

http://www.mcp.com/newriders